The Primary Teacher's Care

CW00542879

The Primary Teacher's Career Handbook is invaluable to all those in Primary education. This essential and unique handbook sets out a complete and much needed career development path for Primary School teachers from the stage of seeking a first appointment, through to middle-management, Headship and beyond. Throughout the book, teachers will be shown how to plan their career development by making their present role successful, enabling them to make a smooth progression to achieve their career aspirations.

Offering realistic advice and including pragmatic solutions, which result from years of first-hand experience, the chapters explore key career stages such as:

- applying for your first teaching post;
- being successful in your induction year;
- managing a subject area;
- professional development and developing as a leader;
- preparing for Deputy Headship and achieving your first Headship role;
- building your CV and making an application;
- interviews; and
- working with colleagues, parents and governors.

Written to support the work of all those in the field of Primary education, this book is not just essential reading for trainee and newly qualified teachers, but it is an invaluable resource for teachers at every stage of their careers.

Keith Richmond is currently Headteacher of Woodside Primary School in Hertfordshire having previously been a Deputy Head in North London.

Richard Greenfield is now an Independent Educational Consultant following thirty-two years as a Headteacher of Primary Schools in London and Essex.

Both also serve as visiting lecturers and external examiners to Higher Education establishments working in the field of teacher education.

The Primary Teacher's Career Handbook

Keith Richmond and
Richard Greenfield

Routledge
Taylor & Francis Group

LONDON AND NEW YORK

First published 2015
by Routledge
2 Park Square, Milton Park, Abingdon, Oxon OX14 4RN

and by Routledge
711 Third Avenue, New York, NY 10017

Routledge is an imprint of the Taylor & Francis Group, an Informa business

British Library Cataloguing in Publication Data
A catalogue record for this book is available from the British Library

Library of Congress Cataloging in Publication Data
Richmond, Keith, 1963–
   The primary teacher's career handbook / Keith Richmond and
   Richard Greenfield.
   pages cm
   1. Primary school teachers. I. Greenfield, Richard (Richard Llewellyn).
   II. Title.
   LB1775.8.R53 2015
   372.11 – dc23
   2014040958

ISBN: 978-1-138-81404-2 (hbk)
ISBN: 978-1-138-81405-9 (pbk)
ISBN: 978-1-315-74776-7 (ebk)

Typeset in Bembo and Helvetica Neue
by Florence Production Ltd, Stoodleigh, Devon, UK

Contents

Introduction

Ask most people and the chances are they will say that they think of teaching as a career rather than just a job. The use of the word 'career' implies a commitment and the idea that there will be some sort of progression of skills and role with time, together with an expectation that experience, understanding, expertise, responsibility and financial rewards will increase over the years.

To a student in the final stages of their training as a teacher, talk of careers and advancement may seem extraordinary and premature when all they really want to do is find a job in a school, earn some money to pay off their student debts, and survive their first term in front of a class without losing control or having a breakdown. This is understandable, but the reality is that in order to succeed in any career it is necessary to plan, and you can't begin planning too early and forming an idea of how you want the next few years, at least, to work out. You need ambition, role models and an idea of what is possible if you are to make the most of your abilities and training. As a student teacher you may not see yourself drawing-up policies, running your own school and leading others, but think of the tyro actor at drama school, imagining their name up in lights in the West End, the trainee barrister picturing themselves as a QC or Judge at the Old Bailey, or the medical student dreaming of being a Consultant in private practice. Why should teachers be any different in their aspirations?

The strange thing about teaching when compared with some occupations is that seldom, if ever, will someone be promoted without actively seeking advancement. In the world of education it's very rare for anyone to be invited in to the boss and told they are going to be upgraded. In fact the system usually works in an entirely opposite way so that the people in charge often assume you are happy and content to do what you are doing unless and until you actively apply for posts and make your ambitions known. The advertising of posts and the selection procedures are conducted according to a rigid process designed and intended to ensure fairness and openness, and usually involve committees of governors and professionals. There is almost always competition for promotions, at every level, so gaining advantage over this competition, and making sure you come out on top, can be a skilled tactical exercise that requires careful preparation and thought over a number of years. Quite often, too, particularly in the Primary sector, promotion involves moving schools and having to establish professional and personal credentials in a completely unfamiliar environment surrounded by total strangers who have no idea about you or your personal or professional qualities, meaning you have to start all over again. This requires motivation, aspiration, self-confidence and awareness, and a will to succeed which may at the time be challenging, or even non-existent, but without which very little of benefit will happen. There's no doubt it also requires a degree of courage and determination.

This book is intended to help you. Importantly, the help it offers is not just for the new entrant to the profession but for teachers at every stage of their careers. There is also guidance and advice here for the experienced teacher seeking to move into subject or phase management, for the middle-manager aspiring to become a Deputy Head, and for the established leader moving to first Headship or beyond. Surprisingly perhaps, certain features in the process of advancement remain remarkably constant at each level of promotion. The questions and challenges may differ but the stages are the same. We offer advice and guidance on choosing a school, the application process and interview techniques, concentrating on how to get ahead and make the best of yourself.

Even if you are dedicated to remaining in the classroom, and have no particular interest in joining management, there are still steps you can take to develop your career that allow you to capitalise on your expertise to your own advantage and to the advantage of others. Being motivated to move, finding the right post, constructing an application, preparing for and succeeding at interview, making an impression in the job, building a reputation and credibility with colleagues, governors, parents and children, all feature in the cycle of career development and the recipe for success. The advice and practical solutions in this book, which result from many years of first-hand experience, will serve you in all of these areas, no matter how 'high up' the hierarchical ladder you are, and will, we believe, make your career progression smoother, more satisfying and more assured.

At each stage of the process you will need to have a clear idea of what you want, what your strengths and limitations are and how to make the most of your qualities. You will need to be aware of how others see you, for example, your colleagues, your 'clients' and your managers, and what you have to offer. You will need to know what to do to compensate for your areas of weakness and how best to maximise your strengths. If you don't know precisely what you want and what you are capable of, you risk ending up in the wrong job, in the wrong school, or being disillusioned and frustrated. The chapters of this book take you through the process and suggest ways in which you can improve your chances of success and avoid the various pitfalls that await those who are unprepared for the exciting opportunities a career in teaching brings.

The book will also prove a useful tool for those in senior positions, or those involved in teacher training or the provision of continuing professional development (CPD), specifically as a means of coaching and supporting the newcomer or the less experienced member of the profession. Each chapter deals either with a stage in the development of a teaching career or a specific challenge such as applying for a job, being interviewed, or returning to teaching after a period away due to family or other commitments. This makes it possible to dip into the book rather than read it as a complete entity, and also means it will serve as a useful companion throughout your life in the world of schools and education.

Whether you are a student contemplating your future in teaching once you qualify, or a Deputy Head preparing to take the first steps towards managing your own school, this book will have something positive and practical to offer you.

1

From trainee to teacher

Comfort zone

If you have trained as a teacher through the School Direct, or the older GTP, route, it will be the case that most of your school experience and training will have taken place in the same establishment. Although you will have had an alternative and contrasting placement, your principal base for the year will have been your host school. Add to this the fact that the school has sponsored your application, employed you as a trainee and, very likely, is somewhere you have worked or volunteered previously in a different capacity for some time, say as a teaching assistant (TA) or nursery nurse, then you have the possibility of a mix of loyalty and a potential conflict of interest that can work to influence your choice of first appointment school.

There will have been numerous advantages to training in this type of climate. The surroundings, the people and the ethos were familiar to you and you feel an attachment to the school. You had the implicit support of senior management and, in all probability, you knew your school-based mentor personally before you started your training and perhaps worked with them, albeit in a different capacity. This meant that you didn't waste time getting used to everyday things, such as policies, working practices and customs, and knowing who does what, and you could use much more emotional and intellectual energy in concentrating on developing your style and technique as a teacher and learning the craft. You will also have had a clearer idea of expectations and who best to go to if you needed help and support.

Make no mistake though; there is a downside to this arrangement. Your experience of schools in general will be more limited than trainees working in other programmes who will have had three, or maybe more, placements in a range of schools that they did not choose and of which they had little, if any, prior knowledge. Although admittedly more challenging for them in many ways, it meant they were able to develop strategies for adapting, for making a good impression on their colleagues and finding their way around a strange setting. While the staff at their schools did not know in advance what they were capable of, they also did not know their shortcomings or make prejudgments about their abilities or potential for success as teachers. With this type of training, there is always an opportunity to learn from your mistakes, respond to advice and to 'reinvent' yourself in each new placement if you feel that your previous one didn't work out as you would have wished.

When changing roles in your host school, say from classroom support to professional trainee teacher, there is always a risk, however small, of inciting envy and ill-feeling among your former colleagues – some of whom, perhaps, might resent what they see as your new status. This may not be usual, and many trainees in this situation report nothing but encouragement and support from others, but you should be aware of the risk and avoid any behaviour on your part that could create a problem. The children, too, will know you in a different role and may take a little time to adjust (for example, in some schools, rather surprisingly perhaps, the support staff are called by their first names and the teachers are referred to by their titles, i.e. Miss, Mrs or Mr). Another drawback is that a TA who becomes a trainee teacher sometimes finds teacher colleagues placing expectations on them relating to their previous role, as in 'you did this or that when you were a TA, why can't you keep on doing it?'. Old habits and routines can persist and this can lead to pressures and conflict which are best avoided or which sometimes require frank conversations and a degree of assertiveness to resolve them. Being forewarned is the best preparation.

The decisions that have to be taken when you are approaching the end of your training and thinking about future employment prospects as a newly qualified teacher should take account of these issues. For instance, if you stay in your host school you may be changing roles within it for a second time, this time from trainee teacher to a qualified one, with all this implies about the need, once more, to bring about a change in the way your colleagues, and others, view you. Some responsibility for how successful this metamorphosis is rests with the school management itself and how sensitively they handle it with pupils, parents and other staff.

Although your sponsor school has a duty to make every effort to offer you a permanent job on qualifying, they are not obliged to do so and there are many sound and practical reasons why it may not be possible, not least that it could be they have no suitable vacancy. On the other hand they may place an expectation on you to work for them on the basis that they have 'subsidised' your training for a year, and they may imply that they see you have a moral duty to repay their support. However, whether you seek a job in your host school or not is entirely a matter for you and the decision should be based on what you see as the best career path and the best means of developing your skills, and not what others think or expect of you. Ask yourself, do you need a different experience, a more (or less) challenging setting for your induction year, or the chance to make an impression on a new set of colleagues as a competent professional? Would you do better making a fresh start with a chance to put into practice all you have learnt without others knowing about any mistakes you have made or difficulties you have had on the way? Alternatively, are you the sort of person who doesn't settle easily or thrive in new and challenging environments? One who needs the reassurance of the familiar and the comfort of well-known faces and established routines? In short, is your host school the best place to develop your career beyond training, or do you need time out of your comfort zone to develop yourself as an independent, free-thinking professional?

Other training routes

Students who have followed the more traditional university-based routes into teaching, either the one year PGCE or the undergraduate BA/BEd course, will have a different perspective on a first appointment. They will have experienced a number of school placements, possibly away from their home town, and may feel less loyalty towards any of them and won't necessarily have any sense of obligation. Although possible, it is less likely that they will seek a post in any of their placement schools and their search for a job will be primarily motivated by factors such as location, type of school or catchment. They will not have had the benefit of being paid while training, which most School Direct trainees have, and so financial motives will probably be in the forefront of their plans. The school experience of these students will in some ways be more extensive and varied than those on the School Direct programme and they may find themselves better placed to make decisions about the type of school that will best suit them. Because of the greater range of experience, they may also be seen by some schools as a more 'marketable commodity'.

These differences apart, the process of choosing and applying for a first post is essentially the same for all those qualifying as teachers and involves planning, thought and judgment and is certainly not something to be rushed into. You may be influenced in your decision by the year group on offer, especially if your practical experience has been limited to a small number of age groups, as is likely for School Direct trainees, but it is important to realise that, as a Primary-trained teacher, you might be expected subsequently to work with any age of children, and you would do well not to limit your opportunities by appearing too fussy at this stage. Instead, versatility and adaptability are desirable qualities that schools will value.

Applying for first posts

The task of looking for vacancies and applying for first posts begins, for many, soon after Christmas in the final year of training. There is an understandable urgency to get things settled, to have a job for September, so that efforts can be concentrated on final practices and assessments, and getting good grades of course. One less thing to worry about!

We are not going to make judgments about the wisdom of making early applications. Individual circumstances will vary and the supply and demand for teachers will change from year to year and according to region, and there is no absolute right or wrong way of going about it. What we will say is that there are, as always, advantages and disadvantages on both sides of the argument that you should consider before acting.

In summary, there are two routes to applying for first teaching posts. Many Local Authorities operate what they call a pool system whereby applicants are screened and given a preliminary interview by a panel of local Headteachers (HT) and, if successful, are offered a teaching post within the Authority that is not specific to a school. Schools in the area will then, over a period, make their vacancies known and will re-interview selected candidates forwarded by the Authority. This is a buyers' market in which the candidates have limited choice about the schools they are offered or allocated. There is, of course, the reassurance of a commitment by the Local Authority that, once accepted, you will be placed somewhere, but with no guarantee where, or how long you will have to wait for things to be finalised. Sometimes, too, the jobs on offer are in the toughest or least popular schools as these can be the most difficult to fill by other means. Because of the uncertainties involved about when vacancies may arise and how many there will be, some positions are not filled until quite late in the year. So it's a bit like being picked for sides in playground football, with the 'best' candidates going first and others having to wait until the end. Probably the only real advantage of this method is that everyone in the pool gets a job in the end and schools generally end up fully staffed.

There is another way though.

The alternative route involves candidates responding to specific adverts for teaching posts placed by individual schools on the web, in the professional press or in local circulars, and many schools still choose to use this medium rather than rely on the 'taxi-rank' principle of the pool. Schools that are not part of the Local Authority, like Academies and Independents, are obliged to advertise in this way, so looking at these adverts can open up a whole new perspective on what is available. Using this approach can, of course, involve having to make many applications and attend several interviews before a post is secured, and there is no absolute certainty that you won't still be without a position in September. It does mean, however, that you are free to choose from a range of schools and to make some decisions about the suitability, and convenience, of each as a first post for you. The big advantage many see of this type of focused application, however, is the greater element of mutuality in the process and the conclusion that both school and applicant will have made a degree of informed choice. You want to work there and they want to employ you! That counts for a lot.

Applying early in the year by this method has some disadvantage to newcomers, in that serving teachers, who may be looking to move schools, are also in the field of potential candidates, and some schools may prefer to appoint someone with experience. This is a risk that you may not be anxious to take, especially if you find the prospect of a repeated lack of success at interview discouraging. Making an early application is not always the best way, and sometimes you might do better by waiting. This can be a dilemma.

The complexities of teachers' contracts and terms of employment mean that they have until the end of May to resign a post before the summer break, so advertisements for September vacancies can still be found in June or even later as schools try to fill posts left vacant by staff leaving at the last minute. However, a school with a vacancy cannot normally offer a post to another teacher from outside at a late stage in the term, because the teacher cannot resign in time to take it up. This leaves Newly Qualified Teachers (NQTs) with a clear advantage as they are free to accept any post at any time, since they are not yet in a post and bound by contracts. This being the case, it is likely that posts falling vacant at the last minute will tend to be filled by NQTs, unless schools are prepared to cover vacancies with supply or agency staff, which most don't view as the ideal solution. It's a fine judgment for applicants to make. Do you apply early and secure a post, even if it means going through the lottery of the pool, or do you hold your nerve, wait until the last minute, and gamble on being appointed somewhere you might judge to be better? The key principle is that once you have accepted the offer of a post it is not the done thing to renege on the agreement if a better offer comes along. People do it, of course, but it doesn't necessarily do their reputation any favours and should be avoided. Similarly, a school or Local Authority that offers you a post is duty bound to honour the commitment, even if this offer of employment is made only verbally.

It's worth remembering, too, that some Headteachers actually prefer to employ Newly Qualified Teachers because they recognise them as energetic, enthusiastic, full of new ideas and open and receptive to training and guidance. They see them as keen young professionals who can be moulded into a particular way of working to suit the school and match its needs. On a more mercenary note, some prefer them simply because they are less expensive to employ, since almost all NQTs now start at point 1 on the Main Professional Scale, which historically was not always the case.

It may also be that the post you are offered is on a temporary contract, for example to cover a maternity leave. Although not always viewed as ideal, there is always a chance for you to impress and to have your contract made permanent in due course. Employment Law prevents schools from extending temporary contracts indefinitely so the longer you stay there and the more successful you are the greater the chance of being offered a permanent position.

Choosing a school

There are a number of different types of Primary School that you might choose to work in: Community, Voluntary, Foundation, Academy, Free School, or Independent School. The differences between them are explained in Chapter 5, but it is important to be aware of the subtleties of these differences, and how they may affect your terms of employment and future career opportunities, before making an application or committing yourself to your first year of work.

Notwithstanding the technical and legal distinctions between types of school, the trainee seeking a first appointment should think about the more obvious differences when choosing where to apply. The first of these is pupil catchment. The area a school serves will largely determine its intake and this has perhaps the greatest impact on a school and its ethos. Schools in deprived areas present staff with particular challenges, but equally so do schools in affluent areas or those with varied and high ethnic mixes or high pupil mobility. Urban schools and rural schools also have distinct characteristics that have to be adapted to. The nature of each of the challenges is different and teachers will need to have, or develop, special qualities, skills and attributes to work in each. You may have a personal preference, or your experiences during training may have shown you that you have particular strengths suited to one type of intake. These should form part of your planning.

The size of a school also has an influence on its character and organisation and will affect the way you are expected to do your job. Across the country, Primary Schools range in size from a few dozen pupils to five or six hundred, or even more. A very small school will have so-called mixed-age classes, where two or more traditional age-groups have to be combined to make classes viable, and will have a small staff, frequently with each teacher managing a range of curriculum areas. Senior managers, including the Headteacher, will possibly have heavy teaching commitments and thus may have less time to support you. The atmosphere will be intimate and facilities and physical resources could well be limited because of financial and accommodation constraints. At the other extreme, a very large Primary School will have multiple 'forms of entry' creating the chance for collaborative planning and teaching between classes in the same year group. Team work will be more in evidence, which might prove helpful to a new teacher trying to get to grips with the workload and range of demands on time and skills. Roles and responsibilities can be shared and there is likely to be a higher number of ancillary support staff. All subjects of the curriculum will be managed by a named teacher, or 'co-ordinator', possibly with specialist skills, to whom you can go for advice. The economies of scale in bigger schools will also make possible a greater range of facilities and resources. The buildings themselves will necessarily be larger and may offer some specialist facilities such as art rooms, ICT suites and group rooms. At the same time, very large schools risk becoming remote, impersonal places and it is not unknown for a Newly Qualified Teacher in difficulties to escape notice for a considerable period if systems of support are not properly in place or if they are reluctant to speak up about their problems.

Some teachers actively seek jobs in Faith Schools. Depending on the religious body concerned, there may be strict criteria in place about who can and cannot apply for posts (for instance, those practising the Faith concerned) and these may be tested by reference or at interview. It is important to recognise also that some Faith Schools can exercise fairly broad control over the personal lives of teaching staff, particularly those in senior positions, so that, for instance, in some situations, divorcees or people in civil partnerships may be frowned upon. It's one area of employment where Equal Opportunities Law does not always apply. Working in a Faith School may be part of your motivation for coming into teaching, and such schools have a lot to offer, but if you take up a post there, you accept, by implication, the codes of expected conduct associated with the religion concerned.

Finding out about a school

It's really surprising how many applicants for posts in schools don't bother to visit them before sending in their application or attending for interview. People who would not dream of buying a car without inspecting and test-driving it first, or purchasing clothes without trying them on, will turn up for interview and be prepared to accept a post committing them to working somewhere with minimal information about the job they are taking on.

Very rarely will a school refuse to allow candidates a pre-visit. In fact, a refusal should be viewed with suspicion, on the basis that they might feel they have something to hide or, more likely, that they are not taking the appointment of a new colleague particularly seriously or recognising the nature of the 'partnership' with the applicant. It is possible, and entirely reasonable, if numbers are going to be high, that visits will be restricted to those shortlisted for interview, or arranged so that a number of candidates can attend at the same time, but courtesy and professionalism demand that some opportunity must be made available and all reasonable questions answered.

Before you apply, there are several sources of information you can access that will help you to decide if this is likely to be the right place for you. The information sent from the school or Local Authority with the application pack is a starter. Read it carefully, looking for clues in the text about what type of person they are looking for and what level of support is on offer. Does it actively encourage a response from NQTs? Are they looking for particular skills, interests or expertise matching your own? What does it tell you about the school, its catchment, its standards and its organisation? Reading 'between the lines' is important. What sort of a 'feel' do you get from the style of documentation: is it informative, businesslike and efficient, or vague, muddled and amateurish?

The next stage will be to search the Internet. Most schools now have a website; draw conclusions and make judgments from what you see. Look at the Ofsted site and read the latest inspection report, examine the Ofsted Data Dashboard to see how well the school is doing compared with other schools locally and nationally, and try to identify its particular challenges and the way it might be meeting them. All these things will affect you, either directly or indirectly, if you eventually work there.

If you are still keen to apply, call the school and ask for an appointment to visit. Again, you can form a view from the way your request is received and handled. Does it sound welcoming or not? Is your enquiry handled just by office staff or are you given the chance to speak to the Head or a senior manager? In short, do you feel, having talked to them, that you want to continue?

Finally, having reached the stage of visiting the school, you should use the opportunity to find out as much as possible about its organisation, ethos, catchment and facilities as well as the level of support which NQTs will be given. Base your opinion on what you see and hear. How does the school feel? Does it look well organised and have a calm, positive atmosphere? Did they know you were coming and prepare for your visit? How do those staff and children you meet respond to you? Do you have a chance to talk to any NQTs on the staff about their experiences? It is important to elicit this information without coming across as too demanding or pushy, and you should remember that, while you are walking around appraising your potential future workplace, others might well be forming judgments about you! The impression you make, even at this preliminary stage, may count in the final analysis, so it would be wise to try not to give too much away about yourself at this point. Something you say, or something you do, or do not do, even the way you dress, can influence those making the decision, possibly subliminally. You may be told that this is not the case, that decisions are based solely on interview responses, but experience and human nature suggest that, for all the emphasis on fairness and equality of opportunity, four main factors are taken into account by the appointing body: the application form and letter; the references; any impression formed prior to interview; and the interview itself.

Preparing your application

We shall look in detail at the mechanics of the application process and writing personal statements later in the book (Chapter 12) because, apart from variations in the nature of the content and the depth of knowledge required, the essentials of a good application are broadly the same, whether you are recently qualified or seeking a Headship.

One of the most important things to remember is that each application you make, whether you complete two or twenty, must appear to be unique and specific to the school concerned. No one reading an application likes to think that they have been sent a photocopied or template letter and a generic application form with the names and dates changed to suit the specific case. Apart from the obvious risk, which happens remarkably often, of omitting to change the name of the school somewhere in the text, it conveys the message that you have not singled out that school for attention but just fired off a salvo of applications in the hope that one reaches its mark. How can you address specific points in the school's documentation if you are using a standard format? It is time-consuming and tedious, but it is essential in order to succeed, and each application must be tailor-made for the job in question, matching the school's Person Specification. Your application must suggest to those reading it that you know the school, that you really want to work there, and have explained why you are applying and what the mutual benefits of you being given the job are.

Interviews

Chapter 13 deals in detail with interviews at all levels, so at this stage we will limit ourselves to things relevant specifically to new teachers. Some of what we say may appear obvious, but our comments come as a result of first-hand experience of selecting teaching applicants as employing Headteachers over many years.

First, dress the part. You are no longer a student; you are seeking appointment to a professional occupation so, no matter how uncomfortable you may feel, dress appropriately. This applies even if, having visited the school, you get the impression that the dress code is a relaxed one. Some staff at the school may be dressed as if ready for the beach, but you should not be. Those interviewing you will want to think that you have bothered and that you are taking the interview seriously and showing due respect to the occasion. If you are smartly dressed this will have the added effect of boosting your own self-confidence and will likely help you perform better.

Second, don't attend the interview unless you are serious about working at the school. There's really no such thing as going just for the interview experience. If the shortlisting process is working properly, you will not have been invited unless they consider you a realistic candidate. Usually the last question you will be asked will be to confirm you are still a firm candidate. You may be offered the job immediately afterwards, and a panel that has taken time to deliberate, having conducted a number of interviews, is not going to be impressed by someone who prevaricates or turns them down. If you change your mind between applying for and attending an interview, let them know without delay that you are not pursuing your application. If, in the course of the interview or immediately afterwards, you conclude that the job is not for you, let someone know immediately so as to allow them to rule you out of their discussions.

Finally, always have a question ready to ask at the end. You know, for certain, that you will be asked if you want to ask the panel anything. Have something ready so that you don't look as if you're unprepared and haven't thought about things. A question about induction support or how you might be expected to work with your mentor is always a safe bet.

Onwards and upwards

After the years of training, the poring over adverts, the intensity and effort of completing applications, and the ordeals of interview, you have finally got a teaching job! Now you can really start building your experience, making an impression and developing your career. This is where the real challenge begins.

Summary and action

Career success requires foresight and planning, and these can't begin too early. There's nothing wrong with ambition. Aim high and plan the steps to your goal.

Certain processes in career advancement do not change very much: the questions and challenges may differ but the stages are the same. Being motivated to move, finding the right post, constructing an application, preparing for and succeeding at interview, making an impression in the job, building a reputation and credibility all feature in the cycle of career development and contribute to success.

Changing roles within a school can be convenient, but moving to a new school setting allows you to learn from earlier mistakes and to 'reinvent' yourself.

When applying for your first post, don't limit opportunities by appearing too fussy. Versatility and adaptability are valued; the quality of induction is more important at this stage than any age-group preference. There are advantages and disadvantages affecting when to apply that you should consider before committing yourself.

Key actions

- When applying for a first post, it can sometimes be better to wait until later in the year. The greater the element of mutual choice between school and applicant, the greater the chance of a good working partnership.

- Be aware of the different kinds of schools. Which type best suits *you*? Remember that many schools prefer to recruit NQTs. Always visit before interview; read the school's website, its most recent Ofsted report and look at the 'Ofsted Data Dashboard'. You are being scrutinised from the moment you walk through the door. Dress professionally and ask sensible and diplomatic questions based on your research about the school. The impression you make, even at this preliminary stage, is critical.

- Give as little away about yourself as possible; this is your only opportunity to interview them and never allow yourself to come across as a *Smart Alec*.

- Ask yourself: how does the school 'feel'? Does it look well organised with a calm, happy and positive atmosphere? How do staff and children respond to you? Could you see yourself being a teacher there?

- Four main factors are taken into account by an appointing school: your application, your references, impressions formed about you prior to interview, and the interview itself.

- Your application must appear to be unique and specific to the school.

- At interview, dress the part; don't attend unless you are serious about accepting the post. Always have some reasonable questions prepared to ask at the end.

2

First steps

Succeeding in your induction year

Starting out

You have finished your initial training course and secured a post as a newly qualified teacher for September. The feeling is great, especially in times when such posts are hard to come by due to the level of competition. If this describes you, then you have overcome the first hurdle in launching your teaching career. As we write this, however, it is very much a 'buyer's market' in some parts of the country and the flood of new teachers applying to schools, each hoping to win a coveted full-time teaching NQT post, means that some are left disappointed. Many of those disappointed candidates end up having to mark time (and risk becoming even less attractive) or enter the growing teacher 'supply' market, with a number of disadvantages for the beginner, and the prospect of delay getting through the induction year before qualified teacher status (QTS) is finally confirmed and the real career-building can begin. While it is true, on the one hand, that a spell of supply teaching can broaden the new teacher's horizons (with little real risk) and provide some much needed cash, the disadvantage of stalling the start of the induction year with little opportunity to get to know the intimate workings of a school, or to consolidate professional learning acquired during initial training, is not so good.

It is our view that the induction year should really be seen as an extension of your training; a time when you can hone your teaching skills in a stable situation with your own class. It is also a statutory requirement imposed by the Department for Education (DfE) that a beginning teacher successfully completes the induction year before permanent qualified teacher status is conferred following a recommendation from the school to the Local Authority. Surviving your initial training, its multiple demands, assignment deadlines, presentations to peers, planning for – and surviving – teaching practice placements is an accomplishment about which you can justifiably feel proud. The induction year as an NQT is a tough, but vital, phase in your career too. In this chapter, we explain how you can make the most of its opportunities.

New teacher

Most teachers never forget their first class. In careers spanning decades, many can recall with remarkable clarity the children's names (especially the challenging ones!), how the classroom looked and what they taught. They often remember the joys and the inevitable lows too. Your first year is special and important. A fulfilling and successful first year will set you up for a satisfying career in teaching, whether that leads you to become an accomplished classroom practitioner over many years, or acts as a precursor to developing in school management, possibly with the ultimate goal of Headship.

First though, you will need to realise that everybody else in the school will expect you to be able to do your job, beginner or not, and to be able to sustain yourself. After all, you might be a 'cheaper' recruit than an old hand, but you are now on the payroll and will be expected to get on with the job. This might sound patronising or blunt; we do not intend this, but it is surprising how many NQTs miss the point about the transition from trainee to salaried practitioner. Your new colleagues will also be under pressure, a fact of life in teaching, and will have limited scope, or willingness, to hold you afloat if things become too much for you. This is why it is crucial that you establish a good working relationship with colleagues from day one and that you take every opportunity to make sensible use of the help, professional development activities and advice that will be forthcoming. Crucially, if you haven't yet attended to it, now is the time to look after yourself, by whatever means, in order to launch your teaching career successfully and to enjoy the unique vocational satisfaction of your new role. Not all jobs can provide such genuine satisfaction: luckily, teaching is one of them.

As an NQT with a first teaching job, you have already accomplished much. Enjoy this feeling. Not everybody in your position will be so fortunate. It means you have a regular salary, and membership of the Teachers' Pension Scheme (TPS) from day one, which we strongly advise you to maintain. Despite recent changes to public sector pensions, the TPS still represents a sound way to prepare over the years to finance your retirement, far off though this might seem! Most of all though, you can finally enjoy the fact that as a beginning teacher you have a class of children that is truly 'yours'.

Holidays

From now on, your holidays will become very precious indeed. While it is true that many teachers spend a good deal of time catching up on assessments and preparing new materials for the term ahead, it is undeniable that one of the 'perks' of the job (probably the only real perk as such) is the thirteen-weeks' holiday from the routine of school that you will no doubt enjoy. You will often face jibes from others who routinely berate the number of holidays teachers get, but make no mistake, you will earn them and need them in order to recharge. Be careful though: too many teachers spend a disproportionate part of their holidays doing schoolwork, and the advice later in this chapter will give you a strategy for balancing your professional commitments with the need for, and right to, a private life. Rather than fend off continual leg-pulling about long holidays, simply appreciate and enjoy this fact, and politely smile and tell anybody who comments about teachers' long holidays that somebody has to do it!

We suggest that you develop an outline plan for your first year, taking each half-term as a separate phase. This will help you in a number of ways: once the novelty of being a 'real teacher' gives way to the realisation that the routine and demands are endless, you can set yourself goals and handle the pace of the academic year with a well-organised and realistic approach that will help you to avoid burn-out and frustration. Essentially, handling the job well means handling it efficiently. You can glean much by observing your colleagues and seeing who is accomplished at this, and who is not so adept. The latter, ironically, often appear to be the most hard-working staff members because it is they who are usually last to leave at night. Appearances can be deceptive however!

Unions

If you haven't already done so during your initial training, join a teaching union. If for no other reason than the legal representation and advice you will have available should something go wrong, it is vital to join one of the recognised teaching unions. There is an irony in teaching, in that there are so many unions representing the workforce that it is, in effect, disunified by the almost tribal differences in political emphasis that each espouses. Just think about the political clout the 400,000+ teachers in England and Wales could have if they were represented by one single union! The major unions and professional associations representing Primary teachers in England and Wales are:

- NUT (National Union of Teachers), which has by far the largest membership;

- NASUWT (the rather quaintly named National Association of School-masters/Union of Women Teachers);

- ATL (Association of Teachers and Lecturers, formally PAT – Professional Association of Teachers);

- NAHT (National Association of Headteachers – represents most Primary Headteachers, although open to Assistant and Deputy Heads. NAHT is also open to Secondary Heads although the majority belong to their own association, the Secondary Heads' Association (SHA);

- Scotland and Northern Ireland, with their similar but distinct school systems, have additional unions to which teachers may belong.

Key steps to a successful and fulfilling induction year

Learn smart

By 'learn smart' we mean to suggest that you can learn from others. There will be no shortage of advice forthcoming from old hands once you are in post. Advice takes many forms and can range from the unhelpful and smug 'that display is sloping downward', to more useful and well-intentioned offers of guidance motivated to help you settle in, and from which you can learn: 'shall I show you how I get going on the children's reports so that I don't spend my half term break writing them all day?' As you gain knowledge and experience, you need to develop a professional 'filter' to separate the useful ideas from the frankly spurious. Nobody has a monopoly on how children best learn and how teachers should best teach. The Government might have you believe otherwise, but the regularity with which policy changes suggests differently. This is why academics have argued over the processes involved for generations, and rightly continue to do so. The best teachers are independent and deep thinkers, learned in their field and open to problematic speculation about what works and why among an innumerable set of variables. You could say that teaching should be seen as less of a technical process and more of an art.

Teachers come in all varieties, as in any other job. There are those who do the bare minimum. There are those who give every hour of their waking day (including weekends and holidays) to the job and yet still find there is even more to do. Then, there are those who work hard, but in a self-disciplined and slick way, and who still find time to enjoy a life outside work; after all, do we live to work, or work to live? Perhaps there will always be elements of both since enjoying life is partly about enjoying what we do for a living. There are no prizes for working out which 'type' we are suggesting you should be. Ironically, those teachers who are habitually being pushed out of the door at six o'clock are quite often the ones who have not learned to work smartly, efficiently . . . slickly. These are the ones who struggle to keep on top of their planning, preparation, marking and assessment and often, as soon as the children go home, spend perhaps too much time wandering around chatting to colleagues.

That is not to say that socialising with colleagues should be avoided; far from it. What we mean to suggest is that the smart practitioner who works slickly will ring-fence times when this is a good idea (break times are always good) rather than allow others to eat into your much needed leisure or family time. They threaten to do this through their own dilatory approach to organising their working life. To put it bluntly, you will have a constant stack of tasks to manage: beware the colleague who befriends you and uses your after-school time to ambush your earlier plan to get your work sorted out and to get home by off-loading their tales of woe. NQTs tend typically to be young, keen to please and friendly. You have been advised! What we are saying is make sure you are the one in charge of your time. If you are happy to drift towards school closing time and then spend all evening with planning and marking, that is fine. If, however, you want to achieve a reasonable work/life balance, you will need to develop a disciplined approach to the working day, week, term and school year. Below, we offer some guidance on how you can manage your time to best effect. It is by no means an exhaustive list, but it will encourage you to think about your new role and to come up with your own ideas on how to work smartly and be happy and successful from the outset.

Cultivate your NQT/mentor relationship

For the new teacher the quality of the school-based induction mentor is key. It is important to form a positive and mutually respectful working relationship as soon as you meet. It is to be hoped that your Headteacher will have carefully selected an experienced practitioner who will be both an exemplar in their own professionalism and pleasant to get along with. Ideally, your mentor will not have been strong-armed by the Headteacher into the role, but will be somebody with a track record of success in their own teaching who wishes to support and induct less experienced colleagues.

As we said in Chapter 1, it is always a good idea to broach the issue of induction and mentoring when you make a pre-visit to a school. The response you get will give you a good indication of the thought that has gone into what is an essential aspect of the recruitment and employment of NQTs. If the answer is woolly and vague, this might be an indication that you should avoid taking up the post. On the other hand, a school that provides a fertile professional ground for beginning teachers will already have good systems in place and the Headteacher should be able to explain them in reasonable detail.

If, after appointment, you are invited to spend time in your new school before the beginning of the term, look at this as a positive indication that your induction is already being thought about by the Headteacher. This is now even more important because Local Authorities (LAs) have gradually reduced, or totally withdrawn, support for NQTs through training programmes. While it is still expected that NQTs will be released from teaching commitments for a half-day each week in addition to the half-day given to every teacher for planning, preparation and assessment (PPA), this is no longer centrally funded and schools have to meet the cost. As well as this, schools often have to pay directly for all additional training any of their teachers attend, including NQTs. In reality, squeezed school budgets mean that such opportunities have been considerably reduced for many new teachers. This implies that the NQT/mentor professional relationship is even more important for the individual's success in their first year.

As a guide, you should clarify and agree the following areas of support from your mentor at an early stage, ideally before the term begins:

- Have an initial meeting with your mentor; set up a mutually convenient time for regular future meetings. As a NQT, you should normally expect to have a formal weekly meeting with your mentor. Agree the start (and end!) times for the meeting. Keep a note of issues discussed and agreed actions and dates by which they should be achieved.

- If you have been given a Career-Entry Profile, or similar document, copy and share it at the first meeting: this makes it clear from the outset what your strengths are and what your professional next steps need to be if your NQT year is to be a success.

- Include some discussion on roles and responsibilities and establish some ground rules acceptable to both parties: confidentiality; times when you can go to your mentor for advice; what to do if you have a problem with discipline or a tricky parent; and so on.

- Discuss how often you will formally be observed teaching in your first year. Every teacher is routinely observed by senior management for monitoring purposes, usually once or, at most, twice each term. This is the school's way of monitoring the quality of teaching and its impact on pupils' achievement. Will your own mentor observations serve both purposes (as a NQT and for monitoring) or will you be observed even more? It is reasonable to expect that you'll be observed up to twice each term, on one of those occasions by your mentor, but to be observed more than this would, in our view, be excessive. Clarify these things at the outset. If in doubt, ask around or, in a case where you feel unduly scrutinised, ask what your teaching union considers to be reasonable. In the rare cases involving competency proceedings being implemented by the Headteacher for a teacher who is a cause for concern, formalised observation will be more frequent. You want to avoid this scenario of course! It's as well always to be on your professional guard too; the seemingly casual visit to your classroom by the Head or Deputy might be just that, but the impression you give will still be noted. Many Heads like to wander around their schools freely, for good reason: as long as you are consistently confident that if the door opens your boss will be happy with what they see and hear, you have nothing to worry about. Indeed, Heads will see your open and friendly demeanour as a positive attribute.

Manage your schedule (pace yourself)

Even as a beginner you will not have any time to waste before getting down to organising and teaching your class. While there is notionally time at the beginning of the academic year to make yourself at home in your new job and to settle into classroom routines, the reality is that your pupils will make no allowance for this. In teaching, the ability to manage one's time effectively is an essential quality for those who wish to be successful and happy in the job. Yet, teaching is also one of those rare professions in which you are a 'trainee' one moment, being supervised by a qualified elder, the next you are managing your class alone and, most of the time, doing so without any supervision. Ofsted, for example, will make no allowance for your limited experience and will use the same criteria to judge your lessons as they do for experienced teachers. There can be few professions where newcomers are expected, unassisted, to perform a range of complex tasks as well as experienced hands, and be fully accountable for their actions, from day one. The sudden jump from student teacher to salaried practitioner is sobering to many and, as we have said, your pupils and their parents will give no quarter here. They will expect you to be able to teach as confidently as any other teacher. It's a daunting prospect for some and one that requires energy, resilience and a certain ability to brave your way through it, at least publicly. NQTs do, though, have the advantage that they are used to being observed regularly by host teachers in their training placements and by their university tutors. This should give you confidence that you know what you have to do in order to impress!

Be an effective time manager

- Keep on top of your marking by assessing pupils' work daily. Never let marking build up over the week if you want a free weekend. Moreover, this is poor pedagogical practice since you need to respond to each child's work and set their next step or to clarify any misconception as the week progresses. This is especially important in hierarchical subjects like maths and English, where the child learns through a sequence of lessons throughout the week or term.

- Develop a self-disciplined approach to organising your day. This includes your own start and end times. Aim to be in school to give yourself enough time to organise your day. As a rule-of-thumb, a classteacher will usually need to be in class by 8 a.m. and Headteachers will expect 'directed time' to begin no later than half past. Often, meetings with parents, whether planned or not, tend to happen just before school session time begins, so this emphasises the need to be in school before any of your 'customers' can come onto the premises – be slick.

- Don't let others distract you! It's tempting to lift your head from marking a pile of books for a chat with a colleague after a busy day's teaching, but it is easy to slide into habitual socialising after school, causing you to get behind in your work and sabotage your evening. If you must have some 'down time' after the children have left, get into the habit of taking a ring-fenced break in the staffroom for a drink and chat about your day with your colleagues. Be strict with yourself: after fifteen minutes you need to be back in class. By being self-disciplined about such things, you will keep on top of your role, feel less pressured overall, and yet still have time to socialise with friends and colleagues without being distracted by them, or distracting them yourself. Perhaps Fridays after school can be reserved for a social get-together with colleagues, ideally somewhere off site?

- Cultivate your professional support network: keep lines of communication with your mentor open. If you have a difficulty or issue, share it with your mentor or other colleagues with whom, with luck, you've formed a good working relationship. It is never a good idea to let things fester; that notorious parent who was sharp with you in the playground this morning is probably the same with everybody else. Another colleague might have found an effective way to engage with them, without losing face, and could offer you invaluable advice about how to win them over. Aside from this, a friendly and supportive shoulder to cry on, as long as it isn't too frequent or burdensome for the other person, is always a good way to deal with the inevitable setbacks that teachers face in their daily lives.

- Organise your professional diary and keep it conscientiously. Your diary, whether in paper form or kept electronically, is your way of spreading the commitments you will have at different points in the academic year. Appointments can be made to fit your weekly schedule. At the beginning of the school year, write into your diary all the key dates, including school holidays, staff meetings, parents' meetings, class assemblies, concerts, other special events, report deadlines and so forth. That way, you will be able to pace yourself by controlling your own commitments around the fixed dates that you cannot control. The best teachers always keep a tight diary, consulting it daily and making additions as soon as they become known: always take your diary to the weekly staff meetings and briefings. Look organised, be organised.

- Do something fun midweek. If a teacher spends every weeknight marking and planning lessons, work becomes tedious and, over time, people come to resent the daily intrusion of work on every waking hour. Perhaps you can be really task-focused after school each Wednesday, since that is the midweek point when you have successfully negotiated three-fifths of your weekly work, and plan to do something for yourself in the evening. The feeling of doing something midweek can make us feel like we are working to live our lives, rather than the reverse. Psychologically, it works and can make us feel contented and, therefore, more effective in our professional lives.

- It might sound silly, but having a plan for your weekend can keep you focused throughout the week. Rather than drift from one week and term to another, develop a habit of planning how you will spend your weekend as a private individual, whether that is socialising, being with your family or pursuing an interest. If you must spend part of your weekend on schoolwork, establish a way of limiting this, for example by working for two solid hours on Saturday afternoon, leaving your evening and Sunday free. Find what works for you and diligently stick to your planned homeworking periods. Teachers who always have their schoolbooks or laptop open on the kitchen table, with the tease of even more work, tend to be poor time managers. Working time effectively bleeds into their private time; it is never far from their minds, and they return to school on Monday not feeling as if they have had a proper rest. This, too, becomes entrenched and levels of energy and motivation become depressed, causing stress over time, and ultimately the possibility of 'burn out'.

- Plan your social diary and trips away from home. With thirteen weeks' school closure each year, teachers are envied for their time away from the job. Having your working year punctuated with enforced holiday times (despite it being exploited by the travel companies) gives plenty of scope to plan those family events, mini–trips and longer holidays away from home. Build these into your diary as soon as they are booked, sharing the emphasis between your schedule of school commitments and personal ones; something to look forward to. Of course, many teachers spend time in their so-called holidays either catching up with their work or planning what comes next. Balance this commitment to work with a commitment to your own leisure.

- Manage your marking, assessments and report writing: there are a number of techniques that will enable you to cope with the permanent demands of paperwork. The key is to be consistent in your application, i.e. do little but often. That way, marking and assessments do not run away with themselves and pile up, which will put pressure on you. Always meet deadlines: for example, if the Headteacher gives 20 June for handing in pupils' annual reports, this is the final date by which they should be ready. Your Head is not there to proof read your careless grammar and spelling; instead, they will be looking at the quality of your judgments about each child's progress and the impression you give through your own professional writing will say much about the quality of your work and also your professional potential. In fact, it is a good idea to begin drafting annual reports, just a couple at a time, soon after Easter, giving you plenty of scope to finalise them and hand them in before the deadline. If you get into school half an hour earlier, say, three or four days each week for a few weeks, you can draft the reports in your normal working day. That way, you will have the Summer half term week to do with as you wish, while your less organised colleagues will be slogging away at thirty or more reports from scratch, in a rush to meet the deadline: work *smart* . . .

- Above all, cultivate a self-sense of being slick as well as conscientious in all that you do. How you actually achieve this is a matter of individual style and preference. But, if you do become a slick operator in your own management of time, you will be rewarded by being seen as a competent professional and, most importantly, you will find teaching satisfying and stimulating; you will be vocationally fulfilled and have a life!

Adopt your own professional 'mantle'

What type of teacher do you want to be? This might sound trite, but it is not. In Chapter 6 we discuss in some detail your own professionalism and how this relates to your continuous professional development (CPD) as a teacher. At this stage, from the first day you walk into the school, think about what kind of teacher (we mean 'professional') you want both to be and to be seen as by others. You may know or work with a teacher whose style and approach you admire and wish to emulate. Although having a number of role models is a useful strategy while developing as a teacher, it can sometimes be frustrating to find that what works for them doesn't work for you. They may be able to command attention with a 'look', while you have to struggle for minutes to achieve the same result. Successful teaching is a subtle blend of technique, skill, experience, knowledge and personality. You have to use a selection of the qualities you have observed in others as raw materials and match them to your personality to construct and shape your own unique 'teacher image'.

Throughout the chapters in this book we encourage you to ask yourself:

- What contributions are you making to the overall life and culture of the school?

- Despite the inevitable highs and lows that everybody experiences, are you thought of by your colleagues as an asset to the school? Or much, much worse, as a bit of a liability?

- What overall impression do you give to your class, all pupils in the school, the governors and other professional visitors?

- Do you act as a good role model in your use of spoken and written English and do you communicate high standards to others by setting them for yourself?

- Do you observe appropriate professional boundaries when working with children, parents and colleagues? Do you know what these are?

- Are you sensible and vigilant about safeguarding, including safeguarding yourself?

- How do you appear and dress? Do you appear as somebody dressed to carry out a professional role and, if there is one, does your appearance comply with the school's agreed dress code?

These essentially rhetorical questions contribute to the deliberate decisions you make about the kind of professional you wish to be. There is an opportunity, when starting out in teaching, to make yourself a 'professional mantle'. Imagine this to be like a magic cloak (there are plenty of precedents) that you place around yourself every time you are being a teacher. It can be whatever material, colours and pattern you desire. Get into the habit of visualising your cloak. When you are wearing it, you afford yourself protection, with your professional self on the outside, and your inner-self, that is, the individual and private self, kept safely on the inside. The metaphor is a useful one. This book concentrates on the steady creation of this professional mantle – your public professional self – and it is during your induction year that this cloth will be cut, shaping your future success and happiness as a teacher.

Summary and action

- Get to know your mentor – establish a common understanding of both parties' expectations.

- Start your professional diary and record every key date you can in advance for the whole school year.

- Accept advice from colleagues, but learn to filter the good from the bad.

- Plan your day, your week and your term: use time efficiently to manage and 'sign post' in advance your essential tasks – work smart.

- Cultivate your own professional mantle: decide what kind of teacher you will be in the whole range of professional characteristics and stick to your intentions.

- Look after yourself: you can be hard-working and professionally committed as well as enjoying a fulfilling private life outside your vocation as teacher.

3

Mastering your subject

What's your field?

Perhaps one of the most frequent questions for you to be asked by other people when they first hear that you are a teacher is, 'what do you teach?' Responding to this as a secondary teacher can be straightforward. Explaining that you teach maths or English, or some other recognisable subject, allows the conversation to flow on easily about the merits or challenges of each particular subject since adults' most recent memories of school are of the secondary stage. They can easily identify with the concept of subject specialism, and almost everyone has a view on whether they enjoyed a particular subject at school or not. As a Primary teacher, the answer can be more challenging. In response, do you simply say that you work in the Primary sector, leaving it at that and allowing the other person to draw their own conclusions about what you do all day in the classroom and how you fill your time? Or do you go on to admit to having to teach around a dozen discrete subjects, letting the other person either marvel at the depth and breadth of your knowledge, or conclude that, if that is the case, you must only have a minimal and limited understanding of each?

The truth of the situation, as always, lies somewhere between these extremes. While undoubtedly a generalist in respect of subject teaching, the Primary practitioner is very much a specialist in the field of cognitive development, early childhood education, and its associated and complex pedagogy, and is expected to have a working knowledge of the whole Primary curriculum. This is something that, sadly, is often overlooked when Secondary and Primary teaching are compared by outsiders, some of whom regard the latter as little more than well-paid child-minding. Compare this argument to a similar one in the field of medicine, about the relative merits of being a General Practitioner or a consultant. Which is it better to be? The answer is, we suggest, whichever you are happier being, whichever you have trained for, and whichever you are more suited to. Each has its skills and challenges, but they are largely different jobs!

The new National Curriculum contains nearly a dozen separate subjects, and there are, additionally, supplementary subjects like religious education, PSHE and citizenship, which will form part of the routine teaching programme in

Primary Schools. As a Primary classteacher, you can be expected, in the course of your career, to teach any or all of these to any age group on a regular basis, and the content and level of understanding required of each can be profound and challenging, particularly in upper Key Stage 2.

In this chapter, we are not going to concern ourselves with how a teacher in a Primary School copes with the demands of teaching a vast range of subjects to the required standards. What we are examining here is how the individual teacher can begin to develop a career with influence beyond their own classroom by becoming the key person in the school who manages a particular area of the curriculum for the benefit of his or her colleagues, whether as a subject specialist, an acknowledged expert or, in simpler and more realistic terms, the person who knows what's going on and what needs to be done – someone who is able to assist colleagues to do their teaching jobs and to ease the burden on senior managers. Not for the first time, we find that the inherent weaknesses in the Primary system, e.g. a relatively small teaching staff, the diverse academic backgrounds of the practitioners, a wide range of subjects to be taught, teacher workload, and a shortage of time away from class, can be used to advantage by the aspiring teacher who wants to make an impact and develop a career.

Who is an expert?

The rise of the Graduate Teacher Programme, and more recently the advent of the School Direct Scheme, has meant that more of the graduates entering Primary teaching have degrees not related in any way to the National Curriculum (business studies, media studies, finance, drama and many more). Although the Post-Graduate Certificate Course, which runs in parallel with school-based training programmes, has traditionally tended to take students with degrees in recognised academic and National Curriculum subjects, the current popular notion of looking upon a degree not as a measure of learning and expertise giving you competence to teach a particular subject, but as a mark of intellectual capacity or potential, means that fewer and fewer teachers in Primary Schools will have degrees that directly help them actually teach any of the subjects required. Consequently, subject knowledge can be at a premium and itself becomes more of a problem to many, and this can be difficult for schools to cope with. Additionally, many of those with degrees in core subjects may choose to go into secondary teaching where they can focus on their speciality without the worry of having to teach subjects where their knowledge may be limited.

Despite being increasingly rare, and perhaps seen by some outside education as lower in status, traditional undergraduate programmes still exist and will continue to train students in a broad range of subjects as well as one or two specialist school-relevant subjects. Here though, experience suggests that, despite the benefits of the more comprehensive theoretical training and range of school placements that such courses offer, many of those coming into the Primary sector through this route have degrees in foundation subjects or early childhood education, so there is still something of a shortfall of degree level expertise in core subjects and science.

Subject responsibility

In most schools, once you have completed your induction year, or soon after, you can expect to be asked to take some responsibility for a subject. This doesn't usually mean a promotion or extra money; it's just part of what happens and it frequently takes the form of an offer you can't refuse! The likelihood is that your first subject or responsibility area will be a relatively minor one and the duties fairly light to begin with, but when the opportunity is presented it is your chance to begin to become recognised and to work towards becoming someone your colleagues respect and go to for advice. It's also a way of developing the skills associated with subject management, such as budgeting, supporting colleagues and acquiring the right resources. In short, it is a way to make an impact and a chance to take your first steps into school management. Don't expect that the subject area you are given will necessarily be related to anything you may have studied at university, or even something you are especially interested in; if it is, count yourself lucky. There may be some element of choice involved, but it is more likely to be simply an area where there is no one else available or one that was previously managed by someone who has moved on. This isn't meant to sound cynical. Primary Schools are immensely pragmatic places and Headteachers need to have all the subjects tied up, with someone, at least nominally, managing what is going on on a day-to-day basis, if only to take the pressure off senior managers and spread the load fairly among the teaching staff. This arrangement will often lead to the situation where a teacher is managing a subject on behalf of colleagues in which he or she has no more specific expertise than they do.

Although there is no standard way of working and schools differ in their approaches, when you take over a subject responsibility in this way, you will probably be called the co-ordinator. Grander titles, such as subject leader, tend to be reserved for promoted posts carrying Teaching and Learning Responsibility payments (TLRs), which, being in short supply for economic reasons, especially in the smallest establishments, are more frequently associated with major subjects such as English and mathematics and jobs in 'middle-management'. Even so, co-ordinators should have a job description and you should familiarise yourself thoroughly with what you are expected to do.

Subject co-ordination in Primary Schools is a complicated area that varies from place to place and is governed by necessity and expediency, so there is no standard way in which things are done. In some cases, subjects are co-ordinated by teachers who have a specialism, i.e. their first degree or main course of study might be in that subject. This is very much the exception though and, most times, there is no such specialism; any expertise there is has usually been picked up 'on the job' or through subsequent CPD. In the main, the responsible teachers act more as facilitators, knowing where to go for information or who to talk to, and look after the administration of a subject. This kind of 'second-hand' expertise is widespread and surprises those not familiar with the running of Primary Schools, but it is essential to the proper functioning of the school, as a way of keeping up-to-date with developments and making maximum use of scarce resources.

Do you want to specialise?

Two subjects in particular in the National Curriculum are different in the way they are viewed by many teachers and are increasingly becoming an exception to the traditional and age-old practice of classteachers in Primaries teaching every curriculum subject. Music and PE have always proved problematic to some teachers, and, unless they have a specialist on the staff who is prepared to take on most of the teaching, schools now frequently employ peripatetic staff, or even unqualified instructors, to work with children on these subjects. As ever, this is a mixed blessing. These people can be employed by the school to do this work during classteachers' preparation, planning and assessment time and it means that classteachers are relieved of teaching two subjects where many might fear their lack of knowledge or expertise could let them or the children down. (The teaching of a modern foreign language, which became obligatory in Primary Schools a few years ago, is, unsurprisingly, also following this trend.) Although welcomed by many, this approach runs the considerable risk of de-skilling classteachers to the extent that, should arrangements change or they move school to somewhere where this facility doesn't exist, they are at a greater professional disadvantage and have to relearn the subject skills and use them once more in the classroom.

If, as a new teacher, your subject expertise is in either PE or music, then beware! Because of the strange relationship many teachers have with these subjects, you may find yourself being persuaded to take on the teaching throughout the school, or at least a large part of it. You are able to spend your days teaching a subject you really enjoy and know about. Good for your status, your confidence, and the respect and gratitude you may earn from colleagues, no doubt, but what about the effect on your longer term career opportunities? Working in this way can mean that you lose a clear identity, no longer having a class of your own perhaps, or not being associated with many other activities that occur in school, and, most importantly, not having a particular reason to keep up-to-date with developments in other subjects. Whereas your colleagues may become de-skilled in one or two subjects as a result of this arrangement, you risk losing touch with many more. You may find that you begin to distance yourself from day-to-day classteaching and the knowledge, experience and skills necessary to function properly and effectively as a Primary generalist.

If you want to develop yourself in this way as a subject specialist in one of these areas, all well and good, and there are definite career routes that you can follow which we discuss later. If not, and you have ambitions ultimately to move into school management, say as a Phase Leader or Deputy Head, you may find the limitations of the experience a handicap. This is because although when seeking promotion you will be able to offer specific experience of teaching a range of ages, with a clear and valuable expertise in your one chosen subject, you may not be able to compete on equal terms with someone who has familiarity with, and has routinely taught, the whole curriculum, even if only to a more limited range of ages. The choice will be yours, but the question to ask is this: do you want to be recognised in a school as the expert on one particular subject, and perhaps be labelled as the person who teaches this across the age ranges, or do you want to become acknowledged as a competent generalist with the versatility to teach the whole curriculum and lead any one of a variety of subjects according to need?

There is no right or wrong answer to this question. The response depends on individual preference and career aspiration, and you will need to plan the actions to be taken that will best lead to the outcome you want.

To complicate matters still further, it is frequently the case that, as they gain experience, teachers will be asked to 'co-ordinate' more than one subject. This arises because of the simple fact that many Primary Schools have fewer teachers than there are subjects of the curriculum, and customary practice dictates that a name has to be attached to each one. This is not as bad as it seems at first because, with experience, the mechanics of co-ordination become simpler and many of the processes involved are the same regardless of the subject. As we've implied, subject knowledge is often a secondary factor in co-ordination, and is far less important than the ability to be organised, versatile and adaptable, and also to be seen to get things done. The main issue here is workload and the possibility of a knock-on effect on quality of classroom teaching.

Valuable support

Although we've suggested that many Primary Schools are hard pressed to find enough teachers to manage all curriculum areas, this is not always the case. Very large Primary Schools can be lucky enough to have a surplus of available talent, and Headteachers find themselves having to be creative if they want to make sure everyone gets a chance to prove their worth.

This means that you may find a range of 'co-ordinating' jobs, which are not directly linked to the National Curriculum and subsidiary subjects, being undertaken by Main Scale teaching staff. In such schools it's not uncommon to find teachers with responsibility for, say, managing the library, educational visits, home–school liaison, or the work of gifted and talented pupils. You should not make the mistake of thinking of these as part of some type of elaborate job-creation scheme, or in any way less important or demanding than work co-ordinating recognised subjects. In an ideal world, every Primary School would have such a selection of co-ordinators. Each has an important contribution to make to the success of the school, and each gives the teacher concerned the opportunity to make an impression and to carry-out a worthwhile task. It may even be the case that you eventually find yourself managing such an area and see in it a niche for being innovative and original and making a difference to your school.

Becoming a co-ordinator

Let's continue by looking at a typical scenario that might occur some time after completing your induction year.

The Headteacher asks you to take on the co-ordination of a foundation subject that is not your degree speciality, say, in this example, history. Although you have no particular expertise, or interest in history, it is a subject that you have, necessarily, taught during your training and first year and that you might reasonably expect to form part of your teaching programme in the future.

You need to familiarise yourself with a number of things. First, look at the generic co-ordinators' job description. If there isn't one, and there clearly should be, ask for one to be drafted or, at the very least, request some guidelines from senior leaders. You cannot do a job properly or have your performance judged if you do not know what you are being judged against. The job description should make clear the limits of what you are expected to do. Are you responsible for drafting a budget, for keeping an inventory, for identifying which resources are required and for ordering them? Is there a subject policy in existence and do you have any responsibility for this policy, for making sure it is complied with and for updating it? Are you expected to have any role in monitoring the teaching and learning of your subject and reporting back to the Headteacher? Might you be expected to lead staff meetings or report to governors on standards in your subject or other aspects of the way it is taught or resourced?

Even though it is very unlikely that you will be expected to do all these things in a first post, this may still sound daunting. You may consider parts of it unreasonable, given your other responsibilities, but it is widespread practice and others in the school will be doing the same. You will have the chance to talk to them about what they do, to compare notes on best practice, and to make judgments about how well they are doing. Although, as we've said, there is every chance that, at your starting level, you will not have this full range of responsibilities, it is worth remembering that when Ofsted turn up (and they will), they may want to talk to you about the subject and the way you manage it, even if only briefly. As usual, they will make no allowance for any lack of experience or expertise on your part, so you will need to become, and remain, well informed.

As we've said, it is probable that you will have little, if any, choice about the subject you are given, but the experience you will gain will be immensely valuable, and you will have a chance to demonstrate your versatility and your ability to study a brief, to take charge of a situation, and to build your subject knowledge. The opportunity to make an impact on learning and to influence your colleagues, some of whom will be senior to you, will pay dividends. The Headteacher would not have asked you to take on a specific responsibility if there were not a belief in, or an expectation of, your capability to cope with the demands. You should not be being set up to fail and you should seek and receive expert guidance, support and encouragement in order to help you develop the role. How well you do, and how responsive you are to advice and challenge, will influence your chances of taking the next step on the ladder and taking on responsibility for leading a major subject or managing a phase.

If you have taken over the management of history and your subject knowledge is limited, you can still develop the role and earn the respect of colleagues in a number of ways. Essentially you are to become a facilitator, not the source of all knowledge. That is, you do not need to know all the answers, and it may be politic to admit this to some extent before you start. Remember, many of your colleagues will be in a similar position and they won't thank you for pretending to be more knowledgeable than you are. Admitting you don't know something can earn respect and support more readily than pretending you do and subsequently being shown to be wrong. To build credibility in the post, you must, however, know where to look or who to ask, and be prepared to respond positively to requests for help and advice. You can expect to be judged by others on your willingness and ability to seek and find guidance when requested. You can take sensible steps to help you with this. Build links with teachers doing the same job in other schools. Liaise with your secondary colleagues who run history departments and who, you might assume, will be subject specialists. Get to know any Local Authority advisers or other 'experts' and get their advice. Watch your colleagues in school teaching the subject, not in a judgmental way, but to inform yourself about best practice and innovative approaches so that you can share them. Talk to your school colleagues to elicit their feelings about the subject, what their worries and concerns are, what resources they lack and how they would like things to develop. Join any local groups of subject co-ordinators to share ideas and learn about each other's successes and difficulties. Look for appropriate professional development opportunities such as local or national courses to develop your subject knowledge or provide guidance on ways to improve your skills as a co-ordinator. Finally, make sure you are thoroughly familiar with National Curriculum sections on your subject at each Key Stage.

All this will take time. You will not become an effective, accomplished and respected co-ordinator in your first week, or even in your first term. Don't become disheartened. By looking at the way others co-ordinate their subjects and, as a classteacher, evaluating the influence and success of their efforts on your own practice, you will learn what is possible and what works. In this way you will become someone whom your colleagues grow to rely on as a source of support and you will find this boosts your self-confidence and willingness to innovate. This collegiate approach and network of mutual support is what keeps most Primary Schools afloat and you have an important part to play in it as a member of the team.

Leading a subject

In some schools, particularly smaller ones, the distinction between a co-ordinator and a Subject Leader can be blurred.

For our purposes, we shall assume that Subject Leader posts are those involving the payment of a TLR allowance and that, as promoted posts, they are advertised, have to be applied for, and may attract competition. In this respect, all that we say elsewhere about constructing applications and attending interviews will apply. Treat any application seriously and prepare well. Make sure the job you are applying for is really for you and that you understand what is involved and what its impact will be on your normal teaching role and your work/life balance. Think about how moving into this job will help to shape your future career aspirations and prospects and what the impact will be on your principal role as a teacher.

We shall limit ourselves in this chapter to considering what these posts involve and how they can be undertaken successfully. It goes without saying that your chances of success in any application will be affected by any judgments made about how well you have carried out any unpaid co-ordination task previously. This is where the impact factor plays a part. If you have done it well, that is, made a real difference, helped and impressed your colleagues and senior leaders by going beyond expectations at times, even if you have acknowledged a lack of deep subject expertise, you can expect to be taken seriously in any application you make and to stand a good chance against any competition.

The job description for a subject leader, say in English or mathematics, will be more exacting than that for a foundation subject co-ordinator. It will almost certainly expect that teaching will be monitored in the subject and that the post holder will possess a certain level of expertise and experience of different age groups.

As a leader in a core subject you will be expected to be aware of assessment results and trends over the years. Familiarise yourself with school data, particularly RaiseOnline, and previous Ofsted judgments, and be prepared to report your analysis and recommendations for action to senior leaders and governors. Any areas of concern identified will certainly involve you, in conjunction with school leadership, in making decisions about possible action, so it's important to be on top of your brief and to form a clear picture of what needs to be done and how improvements might be achieved.

The role of the subject leader, with a still more exacting range of managerial responsibilities, will be considered further in the next chapter when we look at middle-management.

Size matters

Apart from a certain element of lump sum payment, and payments for special circumstances, such as Pupil Premium or special needs funding, schools are largely funded on the basis of the number of pupils they have. Pupils attract more money per head according to their age, so that secondary students are worth more than upper Key Stage 2 children, and Early Years children attract a slight premium over other children in the Primary School. Parts of this seem logical enough. More pupils require more classrooms, more teachers, more resources. Special needs children require additional support. Why is any of that a problem?

There is, however, something of a paradox here of which those running smaller schools will be all too aware. All schools require someone to lead and manage each key aspect of the curriculum, and to an extent, at least, the work involved is constant regardless of the size of school. The money available to pay financial rewards to staff for doing these things is proportionally less in smaller schools than in larger ones, despite the fact that some of the requirements and expectations are constant no matter what size the school is. We've already pointed out that small schools have to double-up (or worse) on the responsibilities that teachers hold if everything is to be covered properly, so that we frequently find teachers managing their class and running two or more subjects as well. Simply because there are fewer children doesn't always mean there is less to do in managing a subject.

Why does this matter to you and how does it affect you and your career development? If you are employed in a relatively small Primary School, and you are ambitious to advance your career, and if one of the factors in your ambition is financial (let's be honest here!), you may have to plan to move schools to achieve your aim. Very few schools in the smaller category (and we would include those with pupil numbers up to 200 or 300 here) can afford to pay more than a small number of TLR allowances in recognition of extra responsibility. The TLRs that are available may tend to go to support what the school regards as key subjects or responsibility areas (like SENCo or Phase or Key Stage management) with the lesser or subsidiary areas having to be managed by Main Scale teachers receiving no allowance. The availability of promoted posts will depend, to a large extent, on staff mobility, that is, how likely those holding them are to seek further promotion and move on. The limitation in the number of available TLRs is made worse if the school concerned has a number of teachers with considerable experience who are at the top of the Main Scale or on the Upper Pay Scale (UPS), where there is no discretion about the payment. Their salaries have to come out of the same pot as the TLR payments. This potential limitation should inform your thinking when choosing your first school and when planning how the early years of your career might work out. Think very carefully about which subject or management areas are more likely to attract additional payments and concentrate your efforts here.

What are TLRs?

Over the years, the Schoolteachers' Pay and Conditions Review Body (STRB), which has traditionally set the pay of all teachers in England and Wales in Maintained Schools, has tried, with limited success, a number of ways to develop a system that fairly and efficiently rewards teachers for any additional responsibilities they may have. At one time there were up to five long, incremental scales, with over a dozen annual incremental points on each, which teachers moved through as their career progressed. Moving up annually was automatic, but transferring from one scale to the next was a promotion hurdle to be negotiated and was usually recognised by the allocation of a particular responsibility. Apart from the length of time it took to reach the top of each scale, the biggest problem was that, once awarded, it was difficult to change the responsibility, and in some cases teachers were being paid for duties that no longer existed.

A series of approaches was tried, variously called, 'graded posts', 'scale posts', 'incentive allowances' and 'management allowances', all of which fell into the trap of not being flexible enough to follow developments in education or to permit easily the recognition and financial reward of younger, less experienced teachers who had shown promise in areas of management.

The Teaching and Learning Responsibility Allowance (TLR), which is what you will find yourself applying for once promotion is in sight, is the latest of the line. It is entirely separate from progression on the Main Professional Scale and was introduced primarily as a way of recognising and rewarding excellent practitioners who wanted to remain in the classroom rather than moving into management. There are some subtle differences from what has gone before. The first, as its name implies, is that it is supposed to be linked to activities directly affecting the quality of teaching and learning in the school. This may sound sensible and obvious, but there were stories in days gone by of the old system of allowances being used as means of retention of staff, to reward trivial responsibilities unconnected to either teaching or learning, to attract male teachers to a predominantly female environment (e.g. managing boys' PE!) or even, in times of teacher shortage, with no identifiable additional responsibilities attached, simply to attract enough applicants. The undeniable need for schools also to have a system of subject and middle-management has meant that the original purpose of TLRs, that is, rewarding good teaching, has to an extent been commandeered in much the way the previous systems of additional payments were. Very few teachers, it seems, now receive TLRs just for being good teachers!

The second feature of TLRs is that, although generally permanent, they can more easily be varied, by negotiation and mutual agreement, once awarded. A teacher can spend a period of time managing, say, English, and then be asked to move to another area. The flexibility this offers is good for both the school and the teacher. The wording of the letter of appointment is important here.

There are two main TLR levels: TLR 1 and 2, with 2 having the lower level of payments. Within a range, schools are able to pay any rate they choose for each TLR, but, importantly, there are criteria attached to the awards. To achieve the higher TLR (which is less likely in many Primary Schools) teachers have to have line-management responsibilities for a number of people. We shall discuss this in a later chapter.

If we look at TLR 2, which would be the first promotion stage, we find that even this is sub-divided according to payment and responsibility. Posts are therefore advertised according to the TLR level they will attract and the payment that will be received, and responsibilities are graded accordingly. This structure can help you to look at a possible career path.

More recently a new TLR has been introduced (TLR 3), which is intended to address further the problem of flexibility. Unlike TLR 1s and 2s, this is a fixed term appointment and can give Headteachers the scope to target a particular area for attention and to give teachers a chance to demonstrate their skills and ability without the risk to the school of a long term commitment that may not be required or may prove unsatisfactory.

When planning any career move by seeking a TLR (or a move to a higher paid TLR) you have to ask yourself a number of questions:

- Do I like and could I work in the school that is advertising the post?

- Is the responsibility on offer clearly stated and one that I feel able to take on, and how much flexibility is there likely to be in the future?

- What level of TLR is being offered and how does this compare with similar vacancies elsewhere? Put simply, could I earn more money for doing the same job somewhere else?

- What does the job specification expect of me? Is the workload reasonable for the TLR on offer?

- How will taking on this additional responsibility affect my ability/potential to be a good or outstanding teacher?

The importance of legacy

These days 'legacy' has come to have a poor reputation in general use as a buzz-word, open to abuse and frequently devalued by its familiarity and widespread, unjustified and sometimes cynical use. In the context of someone building a teaching career, the term may still, we suggest, be used in a valid way to highlight what a particular teacher has done to develop an area of responsibility in their school before moving on to other things. This can be introducing effective innovations, or improving the quality of teaching and learning in a curriculum area. In summary, what was their impact and what are they remembered for?

Many of the methods of working, the practical solutions and techniques to overcome common problems used in Primary Schools today around the country originated from ideas put forward by teachers seeking to solve local problems. Often these individuals were not senior leaders but classroom teachers and co-ordinators who were inspired to introduce innovations that caught on with their colleagues. These were then copied and imitated by others in other schools and so the evolutionary process continued. There's no copyright or patent associated with these ideas, just the satisfaction among the originators of knowing that something they introduced or promoted has become widespread or perpetuated and part of professional 'common property'. This is what we mean by legacy and it is a chance open to everyone working in schools.

Summary and action

The demands of the Primary School system mean that all teachers can expect to be required to move their responsibilities beyond the limitations of the classroom at some stage and become involved in the 'management' of a curriculum area school wide, even though maybe in a restricted sense. In the first stages, these extra duties are not usually rewarded financially, and form part of broader 'teachers' professional duties'. How well you do at this stage can be a marker for your future progression.

The collegiate approach keeps Primary Schools functioning and team work is crucial to success.

Key actions

- Expect to be asked to co-ordinate an area soon after completing your induction year. Don't be surprised if the subject allocated is one you would not have chosen yourself or one you are not especially familiar with.

- Seek advice from co-ordinator colleagues, other schools, and Local Authority advisers, and aim to build your expertise as a facilitator who knows where to go for the answers.

- If you want to specialise and restrict most of your teaching to a specialist subject (say PE or music) be aware that, in the Primary sector, the advantages and freedom this offers to utilise your skills and interest can be matched by the disadvantages of becoming de-skilled in other subjects and remote from the day-to-day routines of general classteaching. Don't overlook the need to keep up-to-date in case you want to revert to classteaching at a later stage or seek management posts.

- Earn the respect of your colleagues by listening to their views and comments, responding to their concerns about resources and facilities, and being prepared to admit what you don't know about the subject.

- In a small school you may find you are given responsibility for more than one curriculum area. The management skills required are much the same but the workload can be higher.

- Versatility is important. The more subjects you have involvement with during your early career, the broader your knowledge base and the more you have to offer future employers.

4

Moving to the middle

Pulled in two directions

A few years ago, the National College for School Leadership (now called the National College of Teaching and Leadership) introduced a course for teachers entitled 'Leading From The Middle'. To some cynics, this rather strangely named programme was taken as something of a parody of the way some schools were run, suggesting a confused situation in which everyone found themselves being guided by people who weren't actually leading the way but rather struggling to find their own path through a crowd, some at the back and some in front. A recipe for chaos perhaps, with no one in overall charge! In fairness, it was actually a well-intentioned attempt to develop leadership skills in those middle-ranking teachers who were finding that the increasing demands of their posts and the lack of formal training and preparation for management were leaving them especially vulnerable in a climate where accountability was high on the agenda and expectations were rising, not least from Ofsted. Such training was long overdue.

For a classteacher, the move to middle-management is a career choice. It won't be forced on you if you are unwilling or unready to take it on, although a sensitive and supportive management might make helpful hints and suggestions, or give you a gentle nudge in the right direction, if they judge you to be ready. On the other hand, as outlined in the first part of the last chapter, you may be content to remain as a classroom practitioner, to develop your skills and expertise in this respect, and to have only limited involvement with other school activities and initiatives. In that case there should be no criticism of your decision and we describe in Chapter 9 how you can progress in this way. If, however, you have ambitions to move into management, you will need to be aware of the opportunities open to you and the best route to career progression. For the purpose of this chapter, we shall consider the role of a middle-manager in a Primary School to involve one or more of the following:

- Core subject leadership
- Key Stage or Phase management

- Special Educational Needs or Inclusion management
- Assistant Headship.

With the exception of Assistant Headship, which implies a major step in the direction of whole-school leadership, and involves moving to a separate pay scale and different conditions of employment, these areas are not otherwise hierarchical. That is, no one type of post should be seen as necessarily superior or preferable to any others, but each will attract seniority and TLR payments of various levels depending on school policy and priorities. Everything is dependent on context. The amount of responsibility attached to each type of post will differ according to the size and circumstances of the school, and the level of delegation that leadership is prepared to accede to and build into the job description. For instance, in the case of the Special Educational Needs Co-ordinator (SENCo) – sometimes called the Inclusion Manager/Co-ordinator (INCo) – the role and responsibilities will be related to the number of children falling into this category and the level of challenge they present, with the workload varying accordingly. For this reason it is hard to be categorical about exactly what each of these posts might involve and we shall limit ourselves to generalities when describing the nature of each post.

The direction in which you move your career at this stage will, of course, be dependent on what is on offer and which field of interest is most attractive to you. It will also be influenced by whether you are prepared to move schools and, if so, how far you are prepared to travel. You will need to judge too how the experience you expect to gain from a post will fit into your career plan and assist any subsequent moves. Will it be limiting, or will it develop your experience in a helpful way? What will this job do to enhance your professional profile and the chance of making an impact with your next application? When applying for any posts at this level, you should clarify what is going to be expected of you by reference to the job description and by asking questions during your pre-visit. This might sound obvious, but it is something that can be overlooked in the excitement of the chase and is difficult to change afterwards. For example, in these posts you might imagine that you would be provided with a degree of non-contact time, in addition to PPA, to allow you to do the things expected of you. That is not always the case and is something to establish early on, and may even form part of a negotiation process.

Subject leader

We discussed in the previous chapter the various roles that subject leaders can be required to adopt and how sometimes the job specification is so extensive that a higher level TLR is appropriate in order to attract the right calibre of candidate. Here it will be sufficient to say that those subject leaders who may be regarded as middle-managers and attract significant additional payments will mostly be managing the key subjects of English or mathematics (or perhaps esoteric subjects like music) and, as such, will be expected to have a good working knowledge of developments and progress in their subject and be able to identify any weaknesses and areas for development. Whereas in a Secondary School a Subject Leader or Head of Department would manage a team of specialist teachers in that subject and would be responsible for their performance management, and even for producing references to support any applications they make, that doesn't happen in Primary Schools. You might judge this to suggest that subject leadership at this level is more of a career backwater than other possible routes, and there is some merit in this view. As we said earlier, there are certain potential career risks attached to becoming too identified solely with a particular subject in the Primary School, of which you should be aware and allow for in your plans for the future. The hierarchy is less clear in this case and there is unlikely to be any direct line-management involved, hence little opportunity to undertake performance management (PM) directly related to your subject responsibilities. That does not mean that a Headteacher will not allocate a certain amount of PM to a subject leader – if only by reason of their seniority – but it may constitute somewhat of an 'add-on' to your principal duties.

On a positive note, a subject leader should be involved in lesson observations and judgments of the quality of teaching and learning in their subject, an activity providing useful preparation for future senior management roles. At the same time, they need to have a good command and knowledge of their subject, the various approaches to teaching it, and an awareness of the resources in use across the whole Primary age-range. This expertise could be used in the course of school-based CPD as a way of improving the quality of teaching.

Phase management

Phase or Key Stage management is a relatively recent addition to the responsibilities on offer to teachers in many Primary Schools, but such posts are becoming more widespread and growing in significance and importance. At the same time they are creating an opening for many young teachers to gain a foothold in management and to learn the skills necessary should they want to move to senior positions. The posts generally involve teachers with class responsibilities additionally managing aspects of the work of all teachers and support staff working in a specific Key Stage (this can include Nursery or whole Early Years Foundation Stage). The nature of the work can be wide and varied and gives great scope for gaining experience, both of the range of ages in the phase and the curriculum. The typical job description involves any or all of the following:

•   constructing and overseeing the timetable;
•   devising duty rotas;

- leading assemblies;
- carrying out performance management of non-teaching and some teaching staff;
- dealing with some behavioural and disciplinary issues as referred by other staff;
- planning and organising whole phase activities (concerts, sports, etc.);
- observing and reporting on the work of TAs and some teachers;
- acting as mentor to newly qualified teachers;
- drawing up budgets for phase-specific equipment and resources;
- being involved in staff interviews;
- analysing and reporting on data;
- acting as a Duty Manager on a rota basis alongside other Phase Managers and senior leaders to be available to deal with whole-school problems referred by others;
- leading phase or Key Stage staff meetings.

The extent to which you will be required to undertake these duties will, as always, depend on the type and size of school and the level of seniority implicit in your post – as, for instance, indicated by the TLR payment. A large school could have three or more classes in each year-group, which could mean, say, two dozen or more adults working in a Key Stage for whom you might have line-management responsibility. Being required to undertake most or all of these duties in addition to any teaching role you may have can be demanding and will test resolve and resourcefulness, but it will be invaluable in terms of the experience gained and the pedigree you will assemble for yourself in preparation for a move to Deputy Headship. It is acknowledged here that some of the activities on the list cannot reasonably be carried out properly without suitable training (e.g. lesson observation and performance management) and the school should make provision for appropriate professional development before requiring you to do these things.

Looking at the expectations of the job (as outlined above), it should be clear that, in order to do it well, you will need to possess a combination of organisational ability, people skills, curriculum knowledge and an understanding of pupil data while, of course, being an exemplary teacher and able effectively to manage a class of children. This may sound a lot to ask but they are all qualities that would also be required in a Deputy Head or Headteacher and the future benefits of such a post to aspiring leaders should be self-evident. Before applying to work at this level you would do well to carry out an audit of your skills to remind yourself where your strengths and weaknesses lie so that you can focus on suitable professional development in advance. At interview, you may be in competition with others who have already undertaken relevant training.

The one potential disadvantage of phase management posts, which is common to some other areas of middle-management, is the tendency for them to become a limiting specialism, especially if you hold the post for too long (i.e. there is the likelihood of getting settled and comfortable in a phase and losing touch with what goes on elsewhere). To counteract this there should, ideally, be a chance within the school management structure for Phase Managers to swap roles periodically, even if for a relatively short period, to allow for a broadening of experience. Thus a KS2 Leader could spend some time leading KS1 and *vice versa*. Many of the leadership skills will be constant, so the main challenges would be working with a new team of people and getting used to a different age group of children. Whether such a thing happens depends on the willingness of school leadership to be flexible and to innovate and take risks, and the extent to which individuals in the team are prepared to exchange jobs and work in unfamiliar territory, but the merits in respect of experience gained are clear. A candidate for Deputy Headship who has both teaching and leadership experience in EYFS, KS1 and KS2 is at a huge advantage.

Special educational needs

As we pointed out in the introduction to this chapter, the role of SENCo and the demands of the job will vary according to the number of children on roll identified as having special needs. It can range in extent from a job to be done during release time, by a teacher with class responsibilities, to a full-time commitment undertaken by a senior member of the school staff. (Indeed it's not uncommon to find schools where the Deputy Head also operates as the SENCo.) Similarly the work will differ according to the size of the school and its intake. In some schools the SENCo will carry out all or most of the support teaching for special needs children, and in others they will act more as a consultant, working in a managerial and administrative way by planning and organising the work of other special needs teachers and support staff, writing reports, Individual Education Plans (IEPs) and Education Healthcare Plans (EHPs) and assessments, and meeting staff and parents, as well as liaising with professionals from external agencies.

Sometimes the post of SENCo is expanded, maybe with a title such as Inclusion Manager or Learning Development Manager, to give oversight of both ends of the learning spectrum including the management of support for more able and gifted children. There is no doubt though that, in any size of school, the SENCo is a key person, with great responsibility, influence and the power to make a difference.

What does not change is the legal obligation attached to the role. The SENCo is the only post in a school, other than the Headteacher, that is specifically recognised in Law and that has exacting legal responsibilities attached to it. Governors of all publicly funded schools are required to ensure that there is a 'suitably qualified' person carrying out this job in their school and, unlike other middle- or senior-management posts, the legal stipulations make the job specification and description of a SENCo prescriptive and formulaic. If you are anticipating becoming a SENCo, familiarise yourself with the responsibilities, which may include any or all of the following:

- identifying pupils' special educational needs;
- co-ordinating the special educational provision for the pupils to meet their needs;
- monitoring the effectiveness of special educational provision;
- securing relevant services for the special needs pupils;
- maintaining records and preparing individual reports and applications for the exceptional needs of individual pupils;
- liaising with and providing information to parents of special needs pupils;
- making sure transfers to other schools are carried out smoothly;
- promoting inclusion in the school and access to the school's curriculum, facilities and extra-curricular activities;
- selecting, supervising and training learning support assistants who work with pupils who have special educational needs;
- advising teachers at the school about differentiated teaching methods appropriate for individual pupils with special educational needs;
- contributing to CPD for teachers at the school to assist them to support SEN pupils;
- preparing and reviewing the information on special needs provision required to be published by the Governing Body.

If your aspirations lie in the field of SEN, then you must investigate the qualifications needed to take on this exacting and important speciality well in advance of any application. Regulations require that all newly appointed SENCos in publicly funded schools have obtained the National Award for SEN Co-ordination.

Choosing this career path can be a useful preparation either for school leadership, or moving into teaching in a Special School. Alternatively, it can be a way of broadening and consolidating experience and becoming a recognised expert in the field. This can be either as an adviser or consultant to a group of schools or a Local Authority, or as a Learning Development Manager in a large school, say as Assistant Headteacher.

Assistant Headteacher

Although arguably part of senior leadership, the post of Assistant Headteacher (AHT) has been included in this chapter because of its borderline position between the two and the way in which typical roles for AHTs mesh with those being described here for middle-managers. A comparatively recent addition to teachers' career structures, AHTs can find themselves in an ambiguous position because of the conflicting demands of their roles and the variety of ways they are interpreted. Sometimes these posts are used as a way of giving financial and status recognition to valued senior staff who have chosen not to move on to become a Deputy, but who carry out one or more of the duties outlined earlier as typical of middle-management, while remaining in a class-teaching role. Other schools see them as a distinct career bridge to Deputy Headship and expand the range of responsibilities accordingly. Occasionally too, you will find schools that have no Deputy but, instead, have one or more AHT posts instead. This arrangement can be used as an imperfect expedient to avoid conflict between potential rivals for Deputy, or for practical financial reasons. If you are applying for an advertised post at this level, our advice is to be clear about the extent of the duties and familiarise yourself with the latest Pay and Conditions Document to see what you can and cannot be required to do.

Although AHTs are paid on the Leadership Scale, their obligatory duties specifically do not include deputising for the Headteacher in their absence. Of course, all sorts of people can find themselves having to stand in for the Head during a casual short-term absence, and many welcome the experience, but long term absence should not be included in this. Nor can an AHT carry out specific executive actions, e.g. the exclusion of a pupil, or the suspension of a member of staff, in the Head's absence. If an AHT is to stand in for the Headteacher in the long term absence of a Deputy, they should instead be given Acting Deputy status and paid accordingly.

Performance management

Nowadays systematic Performance Management (PM), also referred to as appraisal, is an established part of the routine in every school. This includes not just teachers, who are required by regulation to be appraised annually and to have their pay progression linked to performance, but also, increasingly, other staff, such as TAs and administrators. This seems only fair and equitable, as it can be argued that all employees should be treated the same and have the opportunity and experience of discussing their work and progress with a line-manager. More and more schools are introducing a universal approach to PM. This has a cost though. In all but the very smallest schools, such a burden of appraisal will, if comprehensive and undertaken properly, be impossible for the Head, or even the Head and Deputy to carry out without help from others in the team.

Increasingly, therefore, governors and senior leaders are drawing up performance management policies that allow for a hierarchy of staff appraisal, with both senior leaders and middle-managers involved in the process. This strategy has the multiple advantages of spreading the work and of allowing more staff to learn and practise the skills involved, while avoiding a situation where staff are always having their work reviewed by the same manager; not, we suggest, an ideal arrangement. As a middle-manager, you should expect to be part of the appraisal cycle, certainly with classroom support staff, but also perhaps with some teachers. If you feel uncomfortable about this prospect, it may just bring into question your preparedness or suitability to work at this level, and we suggest you should think carefully about your readiness for such a career move and what steps you might take to develop your confidence. It is more likely though that any discomfort will be a manifestation of the sort of apprehension and uncertainty associated with any strange new experience in the workplace, which will disappear as you gain self-assurance and become more used to this part of your job. Some form of training is an essential part of this we suggest.

A few schools have introduced the innovative idea of 'three-person reviews' in which the individual who is the subject of performance management will meet with two reviewers. The lead reviewer will have carried out a classroom observation and will conduct the majority of the meeting, with the second reviewer taking notes and adding prompts and comments from time to time. Although some staff may initially be suspicious of this approach, citing, perhaps, the possibility of bullying, the benefits for all concerned are great. The employee being reviewed actually gains some security from the fact that the interview is not one-to-one and may avoid some of the risk of personality clash or bias. There is also an inherent strength in the 'triangulating' approach, which allows for an element of moderation, along with a reduced possibility of misunderstanding about what was said and any agreed courses of action or outcomes. Experience suggests that this approach to appraisal is generally less threatening and stressful to the person on the receiving end, and does, in fact, mirror Headteacher performance management, which involves appraisal by three governors and an external adviser.

This method allows the lead reviewer to concentrate on the agenda without having to take detailed notes. There is the added benefit that more eye-contact can be maintained without the need to keep looking down to write, a fact that helps to generate an atmosphere of informality. Perhaps most importantly, in the context of this book, the second reviewer is able to observe a more experienced person in action and learn techniques and styles – or in some cases spot things to avoid! At a later stage, they will have the chance to move to leading a review with a senior colleague acting as second reviewer and note-taker. A useful debrief and evaluation can follow, highlighting good practice and things to avoid. Such 'on-the-job training' is, we believe, more valuable than any amount of contrived simulation and role playing in the course of CPD.

Getting the most out of the job

This book is written as a guide to career development and so necessarily focuses on the steps you can follow to allow you to advance through the various stages and to reach the top of the profession, either as a classteacher or school manager, if that is what you want. That said, in the interests of balance, it's important to pause a while and look at the other side of things.

Career progression is all very well, but it should not be an end in itself, and three other elements have to be considered. First, does moving up the ladder of responsibility in any way impair your ability to undertake your main role as a teacher? Taking on additional duties, with their associated demands on time, mental and emotional activity, can have an adverse effect on aspects of your performance and may divert you from the main requirement of being an outstanding and exemplary teacher managing the learning of a group of pupils. The balance achieved in this respect is important and it is a matter of concern for both you and school leadership to keep things in proportion.

Second, you should enjoy what you are doing at each point in your career. Job satisfaction is vital both for your personal well-being and to ensure that you are able to give your best to your pupils and those you work with. That doesn't mean, of course, that you will not have days when you have self-doubts, hate every minute of it, or wish you were back as a classteacher with no extra demands on your time. But overall, taken together, you should feel good much of the time about what you are doing and look forward to going to work. If you don't, then maybe developing yourself in school management is not for you.

Finally, are you looking to move jobs for a positive or negative reason? Sometimes we move to get away from a placement, job or people we don't much like, which can lead to taking an unsuitable post that does little to help ambition. At other times we are comfortable and reluctant to move, but see moving as a way of bettering ourselves or achieving a goal. Our reasons for wanting to move are important and we should always give them due consideration.

These things apply at every level of advancement, and the penalties for overlooking them can be high to you personally and can damage the teamwork of the school. What is the merit of achieving an ambition if you are unhappy in the job, you lose the ability to do parts of it properly, or lack the respect of your colleagues? If you don't like what you are doing, why are you doing it? There is probably an alternative way of making a living. This, it could be argued, makes the case for slow, steady progression in a job rather than 'fast track' promotion, but, we suggest, it's more a matter of keeping a sense of perspective at each stage. A high level of self-awareness is important; knowing yourself, how others view you, and what your limitations are. This knowledge should be informed by your own judgments of your ability and potential linked with those of others; for instance, outcomes of appraisal meetings, together with the informal views of colleagues and friends. This will help to keep your ambitions and aspirations within the limits of what is possible and advisable at each point, and avoid the difficulties of being over-promoted and finding yourself struggling and 'out of your depth'.

The Management Team

One way in which schools succeed in developing a more comprehensive understanding of the processes involved in running a school among their middle-managers and aspiring leaders is by establishing a Management Team. Although varying in composition, and sometimes only advisory rather than decision-making, such a team may comprise Headteacher, Deputy and members of the middle-management (and also, possibly, the Bursar, Site-Manager and Senior TA/HLTA). Apart from the clear advantages in respect of career development for its members, a Management Team serves a valuable purpose of sharing the load of strategic planning, decision-making, day-to-day organisation and crisis-management, while building a sense of loyalty, participation and team commitment. If all are consulted and involved in key decisions, all are more inclined to feel part of the outcome and share in its implementation. They see the whole picture. A teacher who has management responsibility for, say, EYFS, but who is also involved in strategic decisions about whole-school practices and policies, will be less insular, have a greater sense of belonging and be more supportive of change. If you are applying for a middle-management position in a school that is new to you, it would be useful for you to ask if there is a Management Team structure, what its brief is and whether you would become part of it.

Summary and action

Middle-management posts involve a number of specific responsibilities (core-subject leadership, phase management or special educational needs) and you should consider carefully which route is best for you given your interests and your future plans. Some posts may involve appointment as Assistant Headteacher on the leadership pay scale. You will be expected to take part in staff performance management cycles, lesson observations and, possibly through a Management Team structure, to be involved in wider strategic decisions. It may be advisable to undertake appropriate CPD before applying as a way of strengthening your application. This is essential if your interest is SEN where formal qualification is mandatory.

To achieve your goal of moving to a middle-management post, it may be necessary to move schools or even to relocate to another part of the country. Consider how much mobility you are willing to undertake and the consequences of this. If your move is being stimulated by unhappiness or dissatisfaction, take care not to leap into something unsuitable as a result of desperation.

Key actions

• Before applying for a middle-management post, undertake a self-appraisal to assess your own strengths and weaknesses as a way of judging what CPD will benefit you. Consider what's been said about you in appraisals and seek the informal views of others whose judgment you trust.

- Weigh up the extent to which taking on middle-management responsibilities is likely to affect your performance as a teacher. You should not be criticised for choosing to remain as a classroom practitioner.

- If you choose to go down the SENCo route, consider the options for developing your career in ways other than school leadership. Plan to obtain the appropriate qualification.

- Investigate whether there is scope for exchanging posts between middle-management colleagues to allow for broadening experience, and ask whether you will be part of the school's Management Team.

- In the quest for promotion, don't lose sight of the need for job satisfaction and work/life balance. If you don't enjoy what you are doing, something is wrong.

- Always scrutinise the job description to establish what you may be required to do and how extensive your responsibilities will be.

- If you seek an AHT post, decide if this is a bridge to leadership, or more simply for financial and status recognition of your experience and skill as a senior teacher that allows you to remain in the classroom.

5

Types of school

What's in a name?

Although you trained as a Primary School teacher and your main professional aim and interest is to work in schools with pupils of Primary age, you would be mistaken to think that all schools catering for this age group are the same. This is not just a matter of catchment, size or location, which we discussed earlier, but about the way schools are organised, legally constituted and governed. Working in a school as a teacher, or even as a senior leader, you might believe that these differences do not concern you, but the reality is that they can affect many aspects of your work, including pay, prospects, tenure and conditions of employment, and it is important for you to understand the differences involved and what their impact is likely to be on you as an employee. This chapter explains the main differences and how they can affect you.

Towards the end of the Second World War, education services in England and Wales were radically reorganised. The 1944 Education (or 'Butler') Act established a new structure of publicly-funded schools, pulling together the many organisations and bodies that had provided and run schools previously. This legislation recognised and made concessions towards the valuable historic contribution made to education by the 'voluntary' bodies, like the Churches and similar foundations, and sought to include them in a standardised, universal, free system paid for by taxes and rates. All publicly-funded schools were to be financed largely by newly-established Local Education Authorities (mostly co-terminus with counties) and two new categories of schools were to be introduced. These were County Schools (later called Community Schools) and Voluntary Schools, with the latter further sub-divided as Voluntary Aided (VA) and Voluntary Controlled (VC).

The Voluntary Schools were constituted in the trusteeship of a Foundation Body (frequently a religious group, but sometimes another charitable foundation) and were given extensive freedom in Law to manage their own affairs. The Governing Bodies of Voluntary schools contained a number of nominees from the Foundation, and in the case of VA schools they were in a majority. VC schools had some level of self-government, but VA schools were given the greater degree of independence. Although 'maintained' by the Local Authority, which provided an administrative infrastructure, paid salaries and met the day-to-day running costs on a per-pupil basis, the buildings were owned by the Foundation, with financial assistance towards their provision and the maintenance of their fabric being given directly by central Government through grants representing a percentage of the cost. The balance was met by the Foundation or through private funds.

Important freedoms for VA schools included the right to determine admissions criteria, to set holiday dates, to define the nature of religious education and, importantly from the perspective of this book, to act as employers of staff. These rights and responsibilities still exist today and there are many VA Primary Schools around the country. If you take a job in a VA school, your contract of employment will be with the school's governors not the LA. In almost all other respects your conditions of employment will remain the same as for teachers in other schools in the Local Authority, except that, as a VA school may be associated with a religious body (most commonly the Catholic Church, although some are affiliated to the Anglican Church or to non-Christian religious groups), it may be a requirement for teachers holding certain posts to be practising members of those religions and for them to do nothing publicly to bring them into 'disrepute'. Your application may also need to be supported by a reference from a clergyman of that religion. Although not strictly correct, Voluntary Schools have come to be known colloquially as 'Faith' or 'Church' Schools.

Church Schools have tended over the years to be very popular with parents and many have acquired reputations, which are not always warranted, for high academic standards and good pupil behaviour, resulting in a high demand for places and consequent over-subscription. Much of this is self-fulfilling, in that parents who have struggled to get their children into what they see as a popular school, and who may have been asked to contribute through their Church towards capital costs of school buildings, may be more likely to think well of that school and to be supportive of it in a number of ways. This support can manifest itself through strict compliance with a uniform code, support for the discipline policy, financial assistance through parents' and friends' associations, and involvement in volunteer work and out-of-school activities. The parents' support, loyalty and belief in the school can be subtly passed on to the children with a consequent knock-on effect in terms of expectations, behaviour and work ethic. There are sometimes generational family ties with the school, which serve to strengthen links. Parents, children and some staff may know each other and interact outside the world of school because of links with local religious parishes and communities, and this can give rise to a common shared bond, which has the effect of strengthening commitment and loyalty.

In fairness, it must be said that there are many Community Schools that have similarly good reputations and attract the same loyalty and support, and there is nothing inherent in the constitution of Voluntary Schools to justify the way they are viewed by parents or the public at large. In many respects it is an accident of history. Nevertheless, it is a feature of such schools that cannot be ignored. If you work in a Voluntary School, you may come to develop strong loyalty, to feel part of the community it represents and to absorb its traditions and ethos, and many teachers spend their entire careers in VA Schools.

In the case of County (now called Community) Schools, the LA is the employer, controls admissions and owns the buildings, with all funding coming directly from them. Voluntary Schools and Community Schools are jointly referred to as Maintained Schools. (The term 'State School' is not generally used except by the Press). A new category of Maintained School was introduced in 1998, when Foundation Schools opened. These schools, which mostly replaced the now defunct Grant Maintained Schools, have a similar constitution to VA schools, but it is less common for them to have a religious connection. National Teachers' Pay and Conditions regulations apply in all Maintained Schools and, to all intents and purposes, other than the religious and contractual aspects described above, as a teacher working there you should notice minimal differences. All Maintained Schools are required to teach the National Curriculum, to employ qualified teaching staff, and are subject to inspection by Ofsted. Despite the introduction and growth of Academies, the majority of publicly-funded Primary Schools in England and Wales are still Maintained Schools.

Academies and Free Schools

There are a great many similarities between Academies and Free Schools, and for our purposes we shall consider them together. In fact, the three categories – Sponsored Academies, Academy Converters and Free Schools – all have the same status in Law; they are all 'Academies', being defined as Independent Schools funded by the State, but held publicly accountable through legally binding funding agreements. (The term 'Independent' is used in a very loose sense, since they are not at all *independent* of government control, being bound by regulations, having to rely on public funding and subject to inspection.) This category of school was established principally as a way of removing (or freeing, depending on your point of view) schools from LA influence and control by funding them directly from central Government. The Academy movement was promoted politically as a way of stimulating innovation, raising standards and increasing levels of achievement for all children. Critics have suggested this was a casuistic argument based on a false assumption. To date, the movement has proved very popular with Secondary Schools, but less so with primaries.

Academy Converters have previously been successful Maintained Schools – rated as outstanding by Ofsted – that have moved to this status as a result of the Governing Body's decision. Sponsored Academies will have been judged to be under performing schools and will have been compulsorily moved away from LA control, given a new provider or sponsor, and required to become Academies in an attempt to raise attainment. The sponsors can be charities, religious groups, business organisations or even other successful Academies. Free Schools are largely newly-established institutions that have been set up by parents' groups, universities, teachers' groups or community organisations, and are run under the auspices of a charitable trust. This means that, if you are seeking a post in an Academy, you cannot make any assumption about the standard of education it provides, and some Academies, ironically, have themselves recently been found by Ofsted to 'require improvement'.

Academies are able to set their own pay and conditions for all staff, including teachers, and they are no longer under any obligation to employ qualified teachers, other than in the role of SENCo. In reality, of course, most teaching staff in these schools will be qualified, if only for historical reasons, but the option of appointing someone with no training is always available to governors. If you choose to work in a school of this type, you may find some advantage in respect of pay and advancement, the governors not being restricted by the limits of annual increments, but there may be corresponding disadvantages affecting your conditions of service. You may find circumstances in which you are in competition for promotion with someone who has no formal training or qualification. It is possible, for instance, to anticipate a situation where the school appoints unqualified staff because it is able to pay them less than those who are qualified. The employment of unqualified teachers can also lead to other anomalies, whereby teachers with QTS could find themselves working alongside classroom teachers, or even being supervised by line-managers, who have had no professional training as teachers. If this is the case, you will need to ask yourself how you would feel working with staff who have not undergone the rigorous training you have and yet are enjoying the same benefits.

If you work in a Maintained School that becomes an Academy, your employee rights are protected under the Transfer of Undertakings, Protection of Employment Regulations (TUPE), but if you voluntarily transfer between schools (i.e. you take a job in an Academy having previously been employed in a Maintained School) these rights may not be protected. If you move between Maintained Schools, your salary status (i.e. your point on the main or upper pay scales) is transferred with you. This also applies when taking a break in service for whatever reason. This does not necessarily happen in moves to, or between, Academies, and you should investigate this before accepting a post. As Academies and Free Schools are run by a range of organisations, there is no consistency of pay rates, working hours or conditions of employment. Some senior staff may be paid at a higher rate than their equivalents in Maintained Schools too.

Free Schools are often set up in premises not originally designed for educational purposes with the possible limitations on activities that this arrangement might present.

These are all matters that you will have to consider when applying for a job, added to which the position is changing constantly and new regulations and stipulations continue to be introduced frequently, which can alter the status of employees in such schools. You should check the latest developments before committing yourself to a post.

The other major difference you may experience as a teacher in an Academy or Free School is in the content of the curriculum. Neither type of school is required to teach the full National Curriculum, the only stipulation being that the curriculum should be 'broad and balanced'. They are, however, subject to monitoring and grading by Ofsted, although Ofsted inspections now occur less frequently in schools previously judged to be 'outstanding'. Flexibility with the curriculum could translate into the need for fewer subject co-ordinators, which could itself impact on your career development.

Academies and Free Schools are able to set their own term dates and working hours although the longer term implications of this freedom have, at the time of writing, yet to manifest themselves fully. It's fair to say though that VA schools have always been able to set their term dates without any major problems arising, mainly because of the need for some sort of consistency between schools in the same locality and the problems that would arise for parents with children in more than one school.

The funding of Academies is on a par with Maintained Schools in the Local Authority in which they are situated, but is under the control of the trustees and Governing Body. Funding to Academies includes a share of the total budget, which would be held back by the LA in the case of Maintained Schools in order to allow for central administration costs. This 'top slicing' means that the total budget available to each school will be larger than that of the equivalent Maintained School, but management will have to find money to pay for services normally provided centrally by LAs. However, Local Authorities still retain some obligations and responsibilities in respect of special needs provision and other Statutory responsibilities.

Independent Schools

The clue here is in the name: Independent (or 'Private') Schools generally have no links with the publicly-funded education system and are run as businesses, charging fees to parents who choose to send their children to them. There are a great many Independent Primary Schools in the country, and their size, together with the philosophy and standard of education they provide differ greatly. Similarly, the accommodation and the quality and level of resources available to teachers and pupils can vary considerably and do not necessarily reflect the fees charged. Unlike publicly-funded schools, which are monitored by Ofsted and regulated by Local and National Government, Independent Schools are largely at liberty to do and teach what they wish in any manner they choose. They are able to operate a policy of pupil selection using whatever criteria they judge to be appropriate, the most obvious criterion being ability. They are free of any requirement to employ qualified staff or to abide by standard pay and conditions agreements, and these may be subject to negotiation prior to appointment.

If you seek to work in an Independent School you will normally have the benefit of smaller pupil groups to teach, and possibly longer holidays, but you may have greater demands placed on you during term time (e.g. at weekends). In some cases you could be required to undertake additional duties outside school hours (e.g. lunchtime supervision, after-school activities) or even beyond the end of school terms. This should all be clarified in advance. As with Academies, you could find yourself working alongside untrained teachers. Sick-pay provision, pension contributions and arrangements for leave-of-absence are usually similar or comparable to those in publicly-funded schools, but you should satisfy yourself about this before accepting the appointment. Similarly, although some Independent Schools may offer facilities for the induction of NQTs, they are not obliged to do so.

It is possible that there will be fewer incidents of challenging behaviour from pupils in such schools, although this does not necessarily follow, and there are some Independent Schools that provide specifically for pupils with behavioural difficulties. Moving from the Independent to the Public sector may also prove problematic in some circumstances because of different curricular and organisational structures that may be incompatible. It will also be the case that your continuity of service, for pension and incremental purposes, may not always be recognised if you move back from the Independent sector.

Remember also that, first and foremost, Independent Schools are businesses. The ineluctable fact is that they exist to make money for their owners and can, like any business, cease trading at any time. Job security is not therefore guaranteed in the same way it would be in publicly-funded schools and a growing number of these schools have closed in recent years where the 'business' has failed.

Infants or juniors?

Throughout this book we use the word 'Primary' when describing the type of school you work in. We recognise, of course, that there are many schools catering only for part of the Primary age range. Some of you will work in nursery, infant or junior schools, or even 'first schools', which, as the names suggest, have more specific age-related intakes. Most of what we say about applications, interviews, curriculum co-ordination and management applies equally to these schools, but we want to take an opportunity here to look at some of the factors that can influence your work and career prospects.

Perhaps the main drawback of working in a 'restricted age' school is that it can sometimes be seen to limit your experience should you wish subsequently to move to an all-through Primary School. There could be disadvantages, say, for a teacher who has only worked in a junior or an infant school seeking to become a Deputy or Headteacher of a Primary School. The extent to which the disadvantage works depends upon the competition from other candidates (i.e. do they have all-through Primary experience?) and may not always be deemed important by the employing body. It is, though, something we would advise you to be aware of, and suggest that, in order to enhance your credibility and boost your chances, you might seek experience of other phases by, perhaps, liaising with a school of the complementary type or even arranging an exchange as part of your CPD. This may prove easier if, as often happens, you share a site with a 'sister school' and, if relations are good, staff exchanges may be encouraged.

The only other significant difference is one of size. Many nursery and infant schools tend to be smaller, and, as we discussed in earlier chapters, this fact might limit opportunities to develop management skills on a large scale, or the chance of gaining a TLR in order to progress.

Summary and action

Apart from the more obvious differences between schools, such as size and location, there are subtle differences based on the way they are legally constituted and funded, which can serve to affect your conditions of employment or your career development.

Conditions of employment and pay rates are standardised nationally in Maintained Schools, but Academies and Independent Schools are able to make their own arrangements. Unlike other Maintained Schools, if you work in a Voluntary Aided or a Foundation School you are employed by the Governing Body, rather than by the LA.

Where schools are linked to religious organisations, there may be requirements for certain teachers (particularly members of the leadership team) to be practising members of those groups.

The National Curriculum does not apply in Academies or Independent Schools, nor are these types of schools obliged to employ qualified teachers. In practice though, most teaching staff will be qualified (certainly in Academies) and the subjects of the curriculum will broadly mirror those in Maintained Schools.

Key actions

- If you are seeking employment in a school that has links with a religious organisation, check to see if you are required to be a practising member of that Faith and if any stipulations are placed upon your subsequent conduct. This will be enshrined in your Contract of Employment.

- If you are planning to work in an Academy, make yourself familiar with the pay and conditions that will apply to you. If you transfer from a Maintained School to an Academy, it does not follow that your position on the teachers' pay scale will be honoured.

- If your employment history has been in a school serving only one phase, you might find it to your advantage to gain some experience in a complementary phase before seeking promotion in a Primary School.

- Remember, Independent Schools are businesses and can cease trading at any time with no obligation to find you alternative employment. Establish your pension and sick-pay conditions *before* accepting an offer of employment.

6

Developing professionally

Why further training?

In professional circles there are many terms used to describe continuation training. It can be referred to as continuing professional development (CPD), in-service education and training (INSET) or lifelong learning. The teaching profession is no different in this respect. Training of the type we describe in this chapter is not to be confused with initial training, which all qualified teachers have had to undertake, but is necessarily a perpetual process since, due to the complex nature of human cognitive development, no one person or group has a monopoly of 'best practice' in the classroom. In other words, none of us is ever complete in our knowledge about education, how to teach and how children learn. Added to this, the expectations on teachers change constantly as a result of academic research, government initiatives and developments in technology. Therefore, as a teacher, what we will refer to as CPD will become an important part of your professional life. There is some training you will be required to do, as part of directed time in school, and other training you will be encouraged to undertake, perhaps as an opportunity to develop further professionally in your established role. At other times you may choose to take part in training that you identify as useful to your career development and that you will need to seek and secure for yourself, sometimes at your own expense. In education, typical training courses available to practitioners include:

- daytime courses on specific and relevant professional topics (day release or INSET days);
- twilight training after normal school hours;
- longer professional certificates and diplomas; and
- postgraduate qualifications, including Master's degrees and Doctorates.

We will consider the merits of each in turn and offer some useful advice on how you can make CPD work for you as a tool for career-building, as well as to add to your bank of professional knowledge which, in turn, will make you a more effective classroom practitioner. When considering the value of any training course, one thing to bear in mind is the fact that CPD is big business. As quickly as Governments introduce new educational ideas and policies, innumerable training companies react by adding courses to their catalogues, sometimes charging hundreds of pounds per delegate for a day's course. In this marketplace can be found both the good and the bad in terms of quality, value-for-money and professional worth. Training, as we have suggested, serves two main purposes: pragmatic and career enhancing. Our advice will enable you to become discerning when committing yourself to training of different types and will give you a perspective on where best you should devote your energies to serve both purposes.

Training and the 'Bandwagon Effect'

Continuing professional development for teachers is greatly influenced by what might be termed the 'Bandwagon Effect', a phenomenon that results in an upsurge of training initiatives following any change in government thinking or political imperative in education and that can serve to influence the training available to you in the course of your career. This is best illustrated by means of a few examples.

In the late 1990s the Government of the day introduced the National Literacy and Numeracy Strategies. Literacy and numeracy had not, it seems, existed as curriculum subjects prior to this, with Primary School teachers being content to teach English and mathematics as they always had, but now the 'new' subjects were to feature strongly in the curriculum with a rigorous regime of prescribed daily lessons following a centrally determined format. The strategies spawned a vast army of 'consultants', many funded by government grants and employed by Local Authorities, who visited schools to talk to Headteachers and co-ordinators, ran courses and generally dispensed advice to teachers on how to teach the 'new' subjects, many, it has to be said, without entering a classroom. The activity reached a peak with conferences, presentations and workshops taking place all over the country, some involving unmanageably large groups of teachers from multiple schools being inducted into the 'new' practices with almost religious fervour. Inevitably with the passage time, the novelty wore off, the impact and import of these strategies declined and interest (and financial support) waned as new ideas came to the fore, and the show moved on.

When the earlier strategies metamorphosed into the Primary National Strategy (PNS) in the middle of the next decade, a large number of the same experts who had earlier espoused so-called 'literacy' and 'numeracy', reinvented themselves as authorities on the new guidelines and began once more to demonstrate their expertise in schools by leading training and advising classroom teachers. Needless to say, the importance of the PNS faded with time and the Government website finally closed in 2011.

The most prominent new thinking in child welfare in the early part of the new millennium was embodied in the 'Every Child Matters' slogan drawn from the title of an important report on child protection, which was the consequence, in the main, of the notorious Victoria Climbié case. Undoubtedly it contained an important set of recommendations that changed certain professional attitudes towards the care and safeguarding of children, and, again, extensive courses were run by many of the same people who had been involved in earlier initiatives. The 'ECM' agenda, as it came to be known, was frequently cited in courses and documents for teachers – often whether strictly relevant or not – as a mantra covering almost every aspect of Primary education, so much so that it became quite unusual to find a Primary School that did not incorporate the title of the report on its signboard, its letterhead, or at least in its 'mission statement'.

The recent government initiative, promoting phonics teaching, has followed a similar path, with many of the same advisers and experts being reincarnated as authorities on this approach to teaching. The newest version of the National Curriculum promises, once more, rich pickings for providers of training and courses.

Our advice here is to learn from history. We are not saying that new ideas should be eschewed, nor that courses are not often a useful way of keeping up-to-date with developments and research, and meeting and exchanging views with professional colleagues facing the same daily challenges as you. We urge you, however, to look at the way this information and knowledge is dispensed, where it comes from, and how authoritative and valid it is, and to draw conclusions from what has happened in the past. Question the motives and credibility of those who would tell you what to do. Do they have a professional pedigree that leads you to have confidence in what they say? The history of Primary education in littered with initiatives that have been tried and failed, in many cases after great financial outlay and personal commitment by teachers. Ideas in education have a 'shelf-life'. They come and they go, often on the whim of governments and their ministers, and they are open to exploitation by those with an ulterior motive, and can be foisted on hard-pressed and, sometimes, gullible teachers and Headteachers, while those who seek to sell the ideas quickly move on to the next opportunity.

School-based training

Routine training on aspects of learning and teaching is universal in schools. Often this is linked to whole-school priorities (sometimes as 'fallout' from an Ofsted inspection) such as developing children's writing, or their mathematical knowledge, assessment procedures, safeguarding, the National Curriculum and so on. Rarely is this type of training tailor-made for the individual, so a 'fit all' rationale is applied, and the staff as a whole will be required to attend. Such training can take place during INSET days (i.e. the five days additional to pupil attendance days that teachers are required to be available for each year) or during so-called 'twilight' meetings. Twilight sessions, as their name implies, are usually late afternoon or early evening events and, as such, have the potential to catch teachers at their most tired, possibly with a stressful day in class behind them and marking and preparation put on hold until later. Of course, the value of such training rests with its perceived and actual relevance to those receiving it. Some staff may benefit enormously; some may see little point in having attended. One important influence on the perceived relevance of the course is the quality of the person leading the session. Many school-based sessions are led by a colleague who happens to be a co-ordinator or specialist in the focus area and it is important to avoid dismissing these occasions in favour of those conducted by a hired trainer, or 'expert', who is brought in to lead the session.

We should remember that schools are full of experts: teachers and others with a wealth of knowledge, wisdom and experience from which colleagues, especially beginning teachers, can benefit. It is unfortunate that some schools valorise the outside expert at the expense of those who actually do the job on a daily, first-hand basis! There are, of course, some excellent professional trainers: we are saying that you should develop a discerning attitude and keep an open mind. The colleague in your school who, through practice, is showing a major positive impact on standards in writing and children's rates of progress might just have the approach that would benefit you too. Either way, you will do well to form a critical approach to the mass of training and trainers you will encounter throughout your career. If all the training you undertake leads to nothing more than to encourage you to become an independent professional thinker, then it will have been worthwhile.

Remember our argument in Chapter 2 that nobody has a monopoly on understanding education. This applies equally to trainers, a few of whom are in business at exorbitant cost as mountebanks with questionable credentials. Some, it is true, have had successful careers in the schools and are now sharing their expertise to the advantage of schools and their staffs. Others turned to training teachers because they had been unsuccessful in the classroom and chose to make a living telling others how to do what they couldn't do themselves! The challenge is distinguishing between them. Interestingly, in other more established professions (e.g. medicine or law), practitioners are usually considered the real experts in their field, since their theoretical knowledge is frequently applied in the pragmatic, real situation. For a number of reasons, teachers are more usually framed as receivers of hierarchical professional wisdom, passed downwards (by politicians, journalists and many other *soi disant* experts), as opposed to being in the business of practice, which, by its nature, creates and adds to the existing body of knowledge in the field. There are historical reasons for this; it is true (teachers, unlike doctors and lawyers, do not regulate their own admission or professional standards) and it is also true that the Action Research movement in education has provided a counterpoint to such polarisation. However, the fact remains that anybody, and everybody, can claim to be an expert in education, yet teachers who actually practise are rarely portrayed as guardians of collective professional wisdom and find themselves constantly being told how to do the job they have trained for.

Often, teachers who have attended an external course are asked by senior management in school to report back to colleagues for wider dissemination. A brief report about what training was done and what the teacher thought of the quality of the course and trainer is one thing; the frequent expectation that the same teacher should share the content of what they acquired during a whole day or more, though, is plain silly. The trend for 'cascading' training to colleagues is widespread, yet quite how you can achieve anything worthwhile in a necessarily short presentation at a staff meeting remains a mystery! This gives rise to the inevitable question: if it is possible to convey the contents of a course to a group of colleagues in such a short space of time, why does the course itself take a day or longer?

Longer professional courses

Longer, school-sponsored courses are usually linked to your role in school, although there is also the freedom to buy training as an individual, either to enhance your professional profile or simply because an aspect of practice is of special interest to you. These courses are often made available through Local Authorities, as in the case of courses for Middle Leaders, SENCos, Assistant and Deputy Heads' courses, subject leader extended training (e.g. five-day mathematics courses) and so on. These courses are useful in that they demonstrate your commitment to your professional development while giving you an opportunity to step outside your own school and its way of doing things. They broaden your perspective and allow you to interact with other professionals with similar roles. Some would claim that the principal value of such courses is the professional interaction and sharing of ideas that takes place during them.

If you have been given a major curriculum area to lead, regular attendance at subject leaders' cluster meetings and any opportunity to do further training in the area concerned can add to your profile with specialised and potentially marketable knowledge. Of course, further training is likely to make you even better at doing the job – something to be grasped. These courses rarely lead to anything more tangible than a certificate of attendance, but they are worthwhile for the reasons suggested. The quality of training can be highly variable, ranging from inspirational to dire. This is down to luck but rarely will an in-service course have nothing to offer you or leave you even worse off.

Professional certificates and diplomas

There are literally thousands of longer courses for teachers offered by universities and other institutions of higher education (HEIs). These courses range from just a few sessions over half a term to one- or two-year postgraduate qualifications in just about every aspect of teaching and learning. Certificates are one tier lower in the hierarchy of qualifications than diplomas and, interestingly, the main postgraduate professional qualification required to teach is itself a certificate – the PGCE. The traditional PGCE, with its intense one-/two-year programme of initial teacher training has more recently been supplemented by the PGCE(M) course, which includes elements at Master's degree level and, usually, 60 credits towards a full MA which comprises 180 credits in total. Some popular qualifications in this category include the:

- Certificate in Further Professional Study
- Certificate/Diploma in Special Educational Needs
- National Professional Qualification for Headship (NPQH).

The letters NPQH included as a suffix to a Headteacher's name on the school letter-headed notepaper denotes possession of this award, which was made mandatory in 2009 for those aspiring to Headship. However, since 2012, the Government withdrew this requirement, possibly due to the looming national shortage of Headteachers at the time, and most schools now include NPQH in their person specification as a desirable criterion rather than an essential one. To those who were required to obtain this qualification before even being considered as a candidate for a job, this seems to be retrograde. In reality, market forces meant that something had to give, and it was this requirement. The NPQH has survived, though, and has evolved somewhat from its early incarnation. Part of the course requires the candidate to spend a short period in another school, giving them a wider perspective, as well as undertaking an improvement project in their own school, an excellent opportunity for the individual to have a positive strategic impact on their school's overall effectiveness. Some people might play down the importance of the course, whereas those who have engaged with its practically-oriented, rather than academic, tasks and challenges generally speak well of it. Commentators have suggested that the newer, completely overhauled course is more rigorous and relevant and, therefore, a better qualification. Our advice, for as long as NPQH is offered, is for the aspirational school leader to consider undertaking the training in order to secure an advantage over the less qualified competition in the shortlisting stakes. The course is attractive because, while expensive, it is currently partly paid for by a DfE grant with the remaining part of the fee usually being met by the employing school.

Obviously, this is a considerable investment all round so the selection process is rather tortuous as a result. There are various forms to submit, a selection day to attend, and the candidate must be 'sponsored' by their Headteacher, who is also required to submit a detailed statement as to their colleague's suitability for the course. That said, having NPQH definitely gives an edge, even though it is now merely an optional professional qualification, and we still recommend it for

ambitious Deputy Headteachers (DHT) who want to maximise their opportunities as they move towards a Headship of their own.

Even where an individual chooses not to undertake NPQH, we strongly
advise ambitious teachers to study for and obtain a postgraduate Diploma or,
better, a Master's degree in Education in an area that is both relevant to the desired
career path and has intrinsic academic and intellectual interest for the candidate.
We discuss these options next.

Postgraduate degrees

Whatever your ultimate aim – whether as leading (consultant) teacher, curriculum
or pastoral leader or AHT/DHT and Headship – a postgraduate degree is now
becoming a must-have professional badge. The growth of the postgraduate
degrees market, now big business for HEIs, has been phenomenal over the last
two decades. Whereas in the past it was rather unusual for schoolteachers to be
qualified to Master's degree level, this is no longer the case; such is the wealth
of courses now marketed by all of the leading Education departments in HEIs.
Many PGCEs now include an option to 'upgrade' Qualified Teacher Status
(QTS) to include up to one-third of Master's level work. The Government has
promoted these PGCE(M) courses and they now represent a growing number
of new entrants' qualifications. For those who are clear that they aspire to Headship, a further degree is almost a prerequisite, with almost every job advertisement
these days suggesting a further qualification as one of its 'desirable' expectations.
The main Master's degrees applicable to teachers are:

- MA in Education – Master of Arts
- MEd – Master of Education
- MSc in Education – Master of Science
- MTeach – Master of Teaching
- MBA in Education – Master of Business & Administration.

All of these degrees have in common the implication that the holder has achieved
a 'mastery' of their area of practice beyond the level of undergraduate study
required to possess QTS. In essence, Master's degrees give postgraduate students
an opportunity to specialise in a specific academic or professional area of study
in order to improve practice. The designation of higher degrees, as these qualifications are called, is based mainly on the university discipline, or department,
in which study is based. The MA degree, the traditional Master of Arts, is the
most common designation and degrees are usually qualified by a title indicating
the area of specialisation, for example MA in Psychology of Education or MA
in History in Education. Confusingly, those Master's courses with a social science
emphasis may also have the designation MSc. Therefore, it is possible, in some

HEIs, to obtain an MSc in the Psychology of Education, and the precise route will often reflect the candidate's original discipline in which the Bachelor's degree was studied. For example, a teacher with a BSc in Psychology is likely to complete an MSc in the same discipline at postgraduate level. This does not, though, preclude the MA for such candidates and the arrangements for Master's degree courses vary between institutions.

The MTeach degree is the newest qualification here and has only recently been introduced. It has emerged from the political thrust over the last few years to make teaching a Master's level profession across the board. With the advent of 'credit' for a Master's given to courses of initial teacher training, it was inevitable that, in time, this more transparently named course would emerge in the postgraduate marketplace.

The MBA degree has been around for a long time now and is often the preferred choice for aspiring Headteachers who wish to inform themselves about the essentially business-orientated nature of Headship, especially since the advent of delegated school budgets in the early 1990s. The advanced study of business administration in the field of Education is an obvious choice for such individuals and, in turn, has given rise to the shift in leadership roles nomenclature: there are now almost as many Secondary School Principals as there are Headteachers, and the title is becoming known in Primary Schools too, especially where the school has converted to an Academy or the post holder serves as an Executive Headteacher, with more than one school in their care. This trend is likely to continue as Primary School places come under increasing demand and Primary Schools continue to increase in size, with a number exceeding more than a thousand pupils: bigger than some 11–16 Secondary Schools!

Traditionally, 'Russell Group' institutions and the established Red-Brick universities from the 1960s, including the Open University, offered the widest range and best quality higher degrees. This is no longer the case and some Education departments in HEIs that were formerly colleges of education or polytechnics, before becoming universities in their own right, provide high quality courses, with flexible study routes. A number of these institutions have won national and international recognition in the various university league tables for the quality of their research and teaching. Our advice is simple: choose the course that combines the best match to your professional interests and aspirations, taking into account value-for-money as well as the reputation of the institution to which you will have to commit for at least two years, while balancing all your professional teaching commitments and your personal life.

Research degrees

Once you have completed your Master's – and if you have the thirst and stamina for further postgraduate study – there is the opportunity to work towards obtaining a research degree in the field of Education. These are:

- MPhil (Master of Philosophy)
- PhD (Doctor of Philosophy)
- EdD (Doctor of/in Education)
- DEdPsy (Doctor in Educational Psychology).

The last Doctorate in our list is now required by the British Psychological Society for eligibility to register as an Educational Psychologist (previously a professionally derived MSc was all that was required). The DEdPsy is, therefore, a professional course of training, which, like the PhD and EdD, confers on its holder the title 'Doctor'. Most students who initially register for MPhil go on to 'upgrade' in order to submit for the full Doctoral degree. The origins of these research-based degrees is a subject in itself; suffice to say here that the term Doctor is derived from the Latin word *docere*, meaning to teach, and implies that its holder is 'learned'.

The PhD originated in the United States in the first half of the twentieth century as a purely academic qualification and, more recently, gave rise to the professional Doctorates, both in the States and in the UK, such as Doctor of Education (EdD). What is important to know is that all Doctorates require a substantial piece of original research to be completed in the form of a thesis, which leads to a demonstrable contribution to human knowledge in the field of study. In practice, for teachers who choose to undertake PhD or EdD this means developing a new way of understanding – and implementing – an aspect of the learning process or creating a new approach to teacher education, school management or policy.

A Doctoral degree traditionally meant that the holder was considered as an academic equal with any university teacher in their chosen field, and this is still the case, although the introduction of the professionally-orientated Doctorates, such as EdD, means that the holder can be considered more broadly as an expert practitioner in their field. More and more senior leaders in schools are pursuing these high-level qualifications and there is no doubt that the status accorded by the title 'Doctor' can open doors in the professional arena, especially for those with such aspirations.

Funding and finding the time

Completing a postgraduate qualification never comes free of charge for the teacher concerned. Some people ignore this fact when, for whatever reason, they enthusiastically sign up for two or three years' part-time study for a higher degree. At the time of writing, the typical tuition fee for a part-time Master's degree in Education is around £1200 per academic year. Courses usually take two or three years to complete, making the total cost for tuition fees between £2000 and £3500. Factor in the cost of IT, reading materials, travel to lectures and seminars and the other sundry expenses and the true cost soon adds up. However, some schools with the financial wherewithal (and forward-thinking Headteachers) will consider sponsoring a teacher for a proportion, if not all, of the cost of a course of advanced study. This is especially so if the qualification is related directly to the teacher's role in the school, and may also depend on the individual's reputation as a credible, capable, conscientious and committed teacher. Hence the importance of creating for yourself an impressive professional identity as a teacher from your very first day, our message from the very start of this book and one that applies to every level in your career. If you think you can make a case for some financial support from your school, discuss the possibility with your line-manager or Headteacher and, better still, see if you can obtain an agreement to link one of your performance management objectives to achieving a further qualification that is related to your specific school responsibilities. Once enshrined in your review statement, you can build upon this situation and make a convincing argument for the school's financial assistance to continue for the duration of the course (as long as you actually do the study and meet course deadlines!).

Another factor to consider with great care is how you will find the time to study. Each individual has his or her own personal circumstances, some with greater barriers to overcome than others, but an unplanned and flippant approach to applying for a course of study is likely to end in the student dropping out. If you wish to study further, you must devise a plan of action, with built in flexibility if things go awry at any point. Your plan should identify when you can carve out dedicated study time without your commitment as a teacher suffering or your personal responsibilities at home being sacrificed. Nor should you accept a situation that destroys your free time to enjoy life. The key, of course, is about balancing multiple demands on your time. Just as we suggested the importance of working 'smartly' in Chapter 2, the same applies to taking on an additional commitment such as postgraduate study. If your diary is a planned one, with key deadlines and study days earmarked and carried out (particularly during holidays), you can manage this without any disruption to your professional and domestic commitments while still enjoying a good social life absent of work and study. It is entirely possible, provided you plan ahead, you aim to meet deadlines before the actual deadline (this allows for inevitable mishaps in your schedule) and reward yourself with incentives that satisfy you: a meal out, the cinema, a shopping trip, a coffee or glass of wine. By developing a slick approach to tasks, and by distributing and prioritising them accordingly, you can find time you didn't know you had for working and living a private life by reducing wasted or 'dead' time, which is not productive, and as a result can cause you to suffer from stasis. You will know your own preferred mode of achieving your goals – you simply need to exploit these means to good effect. One way of doing this is by mapping your career and training pathway, anticipating workload, spreading it evenly and anticipating critical points or deadlines.

Create a training map: a suggested professional trajectory

One way to consider the practical implications of committing to any training additional to that you will do in the course of your work is to make a plan or 'map', especially once you have applied for a course and have been accepted. What follows is just an example, not suited to everybody by any means, but it illustrates the point. It also takes quite a typical (and real) example in which a full-time Key Stage 2 classteacher with four years' experience decides to begin a Master's in Education studying part-time over a period of two years, with a mixed commitment of evening seminars and written assignments in Year 1, and a 20,000 word dissertation based on a project in the second year of study. What follows is the teacher's plan for Year 1 followed by a tentative sketch map for studying in Year 2:

YEAR 1: SEMINARS AND WRITTEN ASSIGNMENTS

Autumn Term: attend 8 weekly seminars on various topics, including an introduction to carrying out Action Research in the classroom – first 3000 word assignment due 14 January (earmark 4–5 specific half days, 9.30–13.30 during the Christmas break for this). 'Diarise' 3–4 Saturday afternoons during term time for further reading and developing ideas for Assignment 1.

Spring Term: attend 8 weekly course specific lectures/seminars and prepare for first 3000 word Assignment 2 due 20 April (earmark 4–5 specific half days, 9.30–13.30 during the Christmas break for this). Plan 3–4 Saturday afternoons for further reading and developing ideas for Assignment 2.

Summer Term: 5 optional lectures on a range of history topics – select options and commit to diary. Mark in diary 2 × 2-hour undisturbed study periods each week plus 10.00–15.00 on 4 alternate Saturdays for extended reading and preparation for long 10,000 Assignment 3 (due end September). Put in diary 2 × 4-day periods for draft writing, one in Week 2 of summer break, one in Week 3. Week 4 – no study or school work (family holiday). Write up long assignment in Week 5 (Mo –Thur 9.30–15.00 daily). Week 6 – at leisure!

YEAR 2: DISSERTATION (20,000 WORDS)

Autumn Term: attend research methods courses weekly/carve out weekly 2-hour study periods each Saturday *or* Sunday. Attend termly tutorial to clarify area of research.

Spring Term: no further lectures/seminars. First half term: finalise research proposal (to be submitted by 1 March). Second half term: carry out data collection and begin writing analysis of findings – use university library on Saturdays for focused study.

Easter Break: begin drafting report (set chapter target) – work every other day, with breaks in between (10.00–15.00) *or* Wed in Week 1 to Tue in Week 2. Summer Term and Spring half term: draw up timetable for completion of draft dissertation before the summer break. Summer for holiday and leisure: catch up time for draft dissertation if required. Submit proof read text by final deadline date mid-September.

Each HEI has its own course structures we know, but you'll get the idea here, despite it seeming rather too fastidious to plan two years of postgraduate study in this manner. By having a plan-of-action, integrating your study schedule into your teaching and personal diaries, you will:

- know where you are and where you need to be at each stage;
- develop the habit of managing your time efficiently such that it does not encroach on your professional and personal commitments;
- learn how to devote discrete parts of your life to specific periods of time, with leisure and rest in between;
- be able to explain to loved ones why you are doing what you are doing in understandable 'bite size' chunks;
- meet key milestones and avoid missing deadlines;
- practise working smartly and slickly in a way that creates even *more* time for your family and recreation than perhaps you had ever realised!

Fingers in pies – other opportunities for teachers

As your career develops and you gain broader experiences of different schools and roles, you will have the scope to pursue other professionally-related activities, such is the wealth of opportunity in education. Some of these activities may pay you on top of your teaching salary, provided this is outside directed time in school, and some will give you an ever richer professional profile to build into your chosen career path. It is a bit of a standing joke that, these days, everybody who does not actually work in a school seems to be a 'consultant' in teaching, yet there are many ways to provide consultancy for experienced practitioners and this can bring in welcome additional income, however modest, as well as add further strength to your profile. Among the opportunities available to those who are adventurous and want to expand their professional horizons are:

- Tutoring – many teachers do this as a sideline, although you should think about the ethical implications of tutoring any pupil in your own school. This would give you a pecuniary stake in the child's academic achievement and can conflict with the equity with which teachers are expected to treat their pupils.
- Mentoring teacher trainees – if you get the chance to play host to a trainee, look upon this as a compliment from your senior colleagues. While most universities pay the school a sum of money for having their trainees on teaching practice, rarely is this money passed on to the host teacher. It is in some cases, though, and an additional amount can be paid to the host teacher as an *honorarium* or even incorporated in a TLR allowance. You should subtly find out if this is the case in your school.

- Lecturing – with the rapid expansion of school-based training for teachers through the School Direct route, there is a ready market for confident practitioners to run sessions, either on behalf of their own school or after hours, for a fee. This represents excellent professional development and is a sure way of adding value to your CV for that next step on the career ladder.

- External examining – those teachers with appropriate seniority can develop their profile in Higher Education by acting as an external examiner for university level courses in Education, including BA(QTS), PGCE, Diplomas, Master's and even Doctoral courses. This is a little known area among those working outside HE, and the examiner must be qualified at least to the same level that he or she is assessing. A fee is always paid by the HEI for the work undertaken.

- Writing – a number of teachers have made the successful jump into authorship and, as you can see, we would encourage you to do so if you feel the 'Muse' take hold!

Summary and action

Teaching provides a wealth of professional and academic opportunities for CPD and further study. It is possible – desirable even – to plan such accomplishments since they act as excellent stepping-stones to even greater things in your career. The challenges relate to finding the time to devote to coursework and making financial arrangements to cover costs. Look ahead and build CPD into your overall career plan – the sense of achievement you will enjoy is immense and motivational. Teachers are 'experts' in their own right: develop expertise in aspects of the job that interest you, both for career satisfaction and advancement. Each step will open up new opportunities in your career: embrace these and move ahead!

7

Returning to teaching

Spending more time with your family

A characteristic of Primary Schools is the high percentage of women teachers employed. Fewer than one in eight teachers in this sector is male, and with such a high number of women in post, schools have had to do more than most employing bodies to adjust to the requirements of maternity leave and career breaks for family reasons. While it is excellent that such progress has been made in allowing women to sustain and develop their careers alongside their family commitments, the corollary has been that schools have had to adapt their working practices and structures in more and more creative ways in order to accommodate the necessary changes.

In recent times, an increase in the opportunities for part-time employment, the chance to change roles and reduce responsibilities, and the widespread introduction of job share schemes, have made it much easier for women to return to teaching after extended career breaks. This chapter looks at ways in which you can make best use of these opportunities to develop your career and, should you choose, prepare for a return to full-time working without being disadvantaged.

Maternity leave

Unsurprisingly, maternity leave is a familiar feature of the Primary School routine and strategies have been developed to reduce its impact on pupils and other staff and to minimise the loss of career opportunities for the teacher concerned. In the former respect, the rise of teacher agencies has been of enormous benefit. They have often allowed schools to engage high quality teacher replacements at short notice for indefinite periods without the complexities of contracts and notice periods and the difficulties of trying to recruit mid-term, which were a feature of previous arrangements. Increased flexibility in sourcing relief staff has created opportunities for agency teachers to be brought in before the start of the maternity leave so that they can work for a few days alongside the teacher concerned in order to ensure a smooth handover and greater continuity.

One of the biggest problems when teachers take maternity leave is the extended cyclical nature of Primary education. Unlike most jobs, Primary teachers work on an annual cycle, with a new class arriving in September and staying with the same teacher until the following July. Working relationships and expectations are established in the early part of the Autumn Term and successes are achieved over the coming three terms until year-group changeover occurs at the end of the summer. Children and their parents become acquainted with, and get used to, dealing with one professional throughout their time in a year-group. When a classteacher leaves or returns in the middle of this cycle, it can be disruptive for both teacher and class and difficult to establish or retain relationships, working practices and standards. Taking over a class from another teacher part way through the year is never easy and, where the budget allows for it, many schools accept the responsibility for easing the returning teacher back into the role, perhaps by giving them a non-class-based job until the new year starts.

When Deputy Heads or Headteachers take maternity leave, it is normal for the governors to appoint someone with an 'acting rank' for the duration. The Deputy would normally be upgraded temporarily to act as Headteacher and a senior member of the teaching staff would take on a similar acting responsibility to replace the Deputy. Although, as in most cases of absence due to maternity leave, there is still a potential for some disruption, there is an advantage in respect of career development for those teachers who have been upgraded and a chance for them, and others, to see how they cope with the role, albeit temporarily.

Part-time working

As with other organisations, schools are obliged under employment law to consider any requests that may be made by an employee to move to part-time working, especially if this relates to family commitments. Considering a request does not, of course, always mean that it will be agreed to. There are some circumstances, both financial and pragmatic, in which it is difficult or impossible to accommodate someone on a part-time basis: think, for example, of the problems of employing a part-time Headteacher. From a financial point of view, and for a number of additional reasons, employing two part-timers is more costly and problematic than one full-timer and this in itself can be an obstacle. That said, most schools have a number of teachers who have either moved on to a part-time basis, or who have returned to work, following a career break and chosen not to work a full week. Although acknowledging that the resulting problems can sometimes be great, this book is not concerned with the difficulties that part-time working brings to schools. What we want to emphasise are some of the challenges that part-time teachers can face so that, if this is part of your plan, you can anticipate and overcome them.

One potential difficulty arises from the definition of the expression 'part-time'. It can be ambiguous but should not, we believe, be interpreted by either party to mean that the teacher concerned is less committed or works any less hard than full-time colleagues, just that they work fewer days. A part-time teacher should consider themselves to be 'full-time' on the days they work: that is, they should expect to engage in planning, preparation and assessment in addition to their teaching role exactly like their colleagues, but on a *pro rata* basis. The teacher who arrives for work at 8.45 a.m. or who slips out at 3.30 p.m., on the pretext that they are 'part-time', is not behaving fairly with colleagues or the school and, these days, most part-time contracts stipulate not only the days to be worked but also the proportion of the 1265 hours of directed time for which the teacher can be expected to attend. Similarly, it is not unusual to find part-time teachers being required to take on a co-ordination role, albeit with some reduced expectations.

Part-time teachers sometimes experience problems with keeping in touch with school developments (particularly if they do not work on the customary day/s for staff meetings) and a commonly heard complaint is that they did not know something was happening. If, for example, the weekly staff meeting occurs on a day when the teacher is not in school, then an important channel of communication is clearly closed. In this case both the school and the teacher have a joint responsibility to make sure that the flow of information is somehow maintained and it may be that, for important matters, the teacher decides to attend the meeting anyway. (The use of Skype or video-conferencing may seem extreme, but these media could certainly form part of the solution if all parties find it acceptable.) Minutes of meetings should be made available and senior management should ensure that all important decisions are relayed to part-time teachers. This is a two-way process and the teachers concerned must accept some responsibility for making themselves aware.

Working *pro rata* will also mean that attendance may not be required during school training days, or perhaps only for some of them. Again, assuming the content of the programme on these days is important and relevant to the teacher (and surely it should be!) there may be a need for negotiation to make sure all part-timers are present, or at the very least, that some mechanism exists for informing them of proceedings. A committed and ambitious teacher would surely not wish to miss valuable training, and some form of compromise must be possible, for example time off in lieu or extra payment.

Many part-time teachers do not have specific class-based responsibilities. Certainly in larger schools it is not unusual to find them carrying out additional teaching roles, such as covering PPA, teaching specialist subjects or engaging in special needs teaching, supporting individuals or groups of children within a class setting. This arrangement can prove ideal for all parties providing the budget holds-up and certain protocols are observed, in particular those concerning preparation for lessons and marking of work. There seems no reason why a teacher covering PPA should not be involved in these essential elements of teaching, and many schools place this expectation on 'cover' teachers. Similarly, where part-timers are engaged in working with SEN children, they should expect to be involved in assessments, review meetings and discussions with parents. If nothing else, this adds to their own professional development and gives them credibility with parents and their full-time colleagues.

Another question that sometimes arises among part-time staff is in relation to parents' consultation meetings, particularly when these take place during the evening. Some part-time staff might argue against any need to be present if they are not full-time classteachers, and a tradition may have grown-up in a school that they are not required to be there. In the interests of morale and teamwork we would suggest that they should attend, if only as a show of support for their colleagues. This brings us back once more to the definition of what it is to be 'part-time' and how the teacher concerned wants to be viewed by colleagues and parents. The last thing a part-timer wants to be accused of by others is having a part-time attitude!

Jobshares

A solution to the increase in requests for part-time teaching, which also addresses issues around the shortage of school funding, is the introduction of jobshares. If two teachers are looking to reduce their commitments it is sometimes possible to arrange for each to take a share of classteaching responsibility. If this is something that interests you, we suggest you ask yourself the following questions before proceeding and discussing the possibility with your Headteacher:

- What percentage of the week are you prepared to work?
- How well do you think you will be able to work with the other teacher concerned? Do you have similarities of 'style', behaviour management and work expectations, or are your work styles complementary?
- Does your classroom 'style' leave room for the involvement of another professional? In other words, are you a team player or a loner? Are you going to be disturbed or upset by the actions of someone else working in your 'space' when you are not present for a number of days each week?
- How similar are you to your potential partner? Are you tidy/untidy, strict/liberal minded, meticulous about planning/easy-going, a leader/a follower?
- How flexible are you prepared to be about the days you do not want to work? (If both of you want a Friday free to be at home things aren't going to work out.)
- Does the combination of available days and hours allow for an overlap to enable preparation, planning and assessment to take place and to allow you to meet to talk about your paired work?

Experience suggests that there are two manifestations of classteacher jobshares in common use. In one, the two teachers share responsibility more or less equally, each, say, working three days a week with the half-day overlap available for PPA. Under this arrangement there is still a need for meetings outside school hours, unless the school is prepared to provide additional cover for this half day. The obvious disadvantage of this is that the class will then experience three teachers each week. The second approach involves one of the teachers having a relatively minor role; for example, teaching for only one day of the week. Although the children will rapidly adapt to either scenario, the latter tends to imply to them that the minor role teacher is less 'in charge' and this may give rise to difficulties.

Whichever option you choose can present a range of problems that you would be well to anticipate and plan to overcome. For example, who writes the reports and assessments? How do you manage parents' meetings? Working fixed days can mean that you might regularly teach the same minority subjects. Is this good for your future career development? You will be working very closely with your jobshare partner for up to a year. Just like going on holiday with friends, this can sometimes be a disaster. You never really know someone until you have worked this closely with them (especially in the confines of a classroom with a challenging group of children) and misery beckons at the prospect of working for an extended period with a colleague whose views on teaching and class-room management are the total opposite of yours and with whom you find co-operation difficult. Apart from anything else, the impact on the children of lack of continuity and poor working relationships between their teachers that might result can be serious and damaging to their progress.

The issues described above apply equally when the jobshare involves a more senior or management post and, in some instances, the consequences of a mismatch can be still more severe. Jobsharing Deputy Heads are by no means unknown and there are even some Headteachers in this situation. The difficulties that can arise in respect of those whose work involves making sometimes far-reaching executive decisions when only working for part of the week may well be imagined, and a clearly defined and agreed set of rules and protocols is essential if things are to work well. There are great opportunities for misunderstanding and confusion among staff, parents and children, particularly about who actually is in charge at any given point and how binding certain decisions are when made by one person without collaboration.

Longer career breaks

Returning to teaching after a long career break brings its own problems for the individual concerned. Going back to any job after a period away is difficult; teaching is no exception. First, it is necessary to get back into the routine, and this is not always as easy as it might seem. Second, there will inevitably have been changes in the interim: changes in the curriculum, changes in approaches to planning, teaching and assessment, and developments in areas like the use of classroom technology. It might well be construed as arrogant to assume that you can walk back into a classroom and simply carry on where you left off, particularly if you have had an absence of several years.

There are ways of preparing for a return, which will lessen the impact on you and make the whole exercise more effective for all concerned. It can, for instance, be useful to acclimatise yourself by taking on some cover teaching beforehand, attending for a few days here and there initially and gradually building up until you feel ready to take on more regular work. You can do this in three ways: you can register with a commercial teaching agency; you can get involved with the supply pool of your Local Authority, if it still operates one; or you can approach an individual school (or schools) and ask to be offered any supply work they may have available. It is important to be aware of the essential difference between 'agency' work and 'supply' work. In the former you will be employed on a casual basis by a private company, which will pay you a standard daily rate irrespective of your experience. Any conditions of employment are determined by the agency and you are simply allocated to a school. When you are engaged as a supply teacher, either by the LA as part of a pool, or directly by the school, you will have a temporary contract, be bound by teachers' conditions of service and normally be paid at a rate related to your last position on the pay scale. In neither case will you be paid for holidays although, as a supply teacher, there will normally be a deduction made towards your pension contribution and the work you do will count towards your 'reckonable' service. A consequence of these differences is that some Headteachers prefer to employ agency staff, as they can be less expensive, with no on-costs, and, because there is a fixed rate, easier to budget for. Some schools do, however, employ regular supply teachers, people they know and trust, even though the employment costs can be much higher in the case of experienced teachers paid on higher salary scale points.

Whichever approach you choose should not be regarded as an easy option. Although, as a casual employee, it is unlikely that you will be expected to attend staff meetings, parents' evenings or INSET days, you will not be popular, or probably asked back, if you regularly leave the premises at the same time as the children without completing your marking and writing a summary of the work you have done that day.

Cover teaching is certainly a way of re-establishing the routine of working in a school, although it can be challenging for the returning teacher, especially if you choose to work in a number of schools or take whatever work is offered. You may find you have little planning or preparation to go on and that you have no idea of the children's abilities or of the school's expectations and that you are largely left to your own devices.

Helping out

Some teachers who are planning to return to the classroom find that working as a volunteer in a school is a helpful way of re-establishing themselves. Although not paid, and relatively low in status, the role of classroom helper has the benefit of having no real commitments or responsibilities. Working in this way can give the returner an insight into any changes in curriculum or teaching methods, the chance to observe different teachers at work in an unthreatening manner, and also the opportunity to work in a range of year groups with which perhaps they are unfamiliar.

If you do this and the Headteacher is aware that you are a qualified teacher, there is always the possibility that you may be asked to take on some paid cover work and that way you will find it possible to work your way back into the system. Many successful returns to regular teaching have been achieved through this route.

Catching up

Throughout this chapter we have hinted that returning to teaching after a break is made harder because of changes that will have occurred in education in the intervening period. The curriculum, teaching methods, ways in which progress is measured and assessed have all changed considerably in recent years and there seems to be no sign of the pace of change slowing down. If, when returning to work, you hope to make your mark once more as a 'good' or 'outstanding' teacher, to use Ofsted's words, we suggest that it would be naïve, at least, to think that you can catch up with developments without reading yourself back into the job and finding out what is happening. No true professional would do this. What we suggest is that you complement the practical experience we have discussed above with some theoretical knowledge, which you can gain by reading the professional press or by attending one or more of the courses for returning teachers that are run by LAs and similar bodies around the country.

Apart from making your eventual return more successful and fulfilling, these steps will help to enhance your professional profile and any appointing body will take account of measures you have taken to keep up-to-date.

Summary and key actions

Maternity leave or longer term absence for family reasons should not herald or bring an end to your teaching career. There are many ways to get back into the classroom.

A move to part-time working may provide an answer but you should not fall into the trap of considering it an easy option. You will be working full-time during the hours you are at school.

- Think about staging your return by volunteering or taking on supply work as a way of getting back into a routine.
- Jobshares can work if they are carefully planned and if the participants are compatible.
- Think carefully about how the arrangement will work and whether it will suit your style of working.
- Don't overlook the need to keep in touch with research and development. Read the professional press and investigate if there are courses to help you return to work.

8

Working with other adults

These days the job of a classteacher involves forming working relationships with a number of other people and is no longer the solitary occupation it once was. The days when a teacher spent all their working time in the company of thirty plus children without the benefit of extra adult support have passed and many classrooms are now busy places filled with support workers each with a distinct and important role to fulfill. Nevertheless, the classteacher is still in charge of what happens and has a supervisory role in respect of other workers in the classroom, even, it should be said, those who are also teachers. This chapter looks at the different types of working relationships that a teacher will have to form and considers each from the perspective of career development. How can you enhance your career and build a good, professional image by the way you interact with other people you come into contact with in your working life?

Classroom support

Partly as a result of the initiative of 'inclusion', but also a consequence of better funding and a change in the way Primary teaching is viewed, most teachers nowadays find that they have regular adult support in their classroom. This support can be used to target individual children or to work with groups of children, but most teachers welcome it. The challenge to the classteacher comes from getting accustomed to having other adults present, using the support well and in ensuring that working relationships are established and maintained.

Managing the work of classroom supporters and volunteers effectively is a skill that has to be learned and the techniques that are used will serve teachers in good stead in any future career in leadership. First, it is important to have a clear understanding of what you want them to do and what their defined role is. Teaching Assistants should have job descriptions, as should any teachers who work in support of specific pupils, and some degree of joint planning would appear to be an essential requirement. Although there should be a tacit under-standing that the classteacher is 'in charge', relationships will be built through a tendency for everyone to be treated as equal partners. The children and any parent helpers will quickly pick up on differences in status, especially those that may sour relationships.

Above all, the work of classroom support staff must be acknowledged and valued by being recognised as an activity that serves both to improve the quality of education for the children and to make the life of the teacher easier.

Parent helpers

Many schools encourage parents to offer their help in classrooms on a voluntary basis. There are many reasons why this is a good thing; their particular skills can be made use of (cooking and art work come to mind); the adult–pupil ratio is reduced, which can be especially important in classes of younger children; parents get to see what the life of a teacher can be like and how challenging the job can be, and this can sometimes lead to them being more supportive and understanding when or if things go wrong.

There can also be difficulties. This is especially so if a parent's motive for offering to help is to have a closer view of their own child's activities in the classroom, perhaps fuelled by some sort of dissatisfaction or worry about bullying or teaching methods. Schools address this problem in some subtle ways. Particularly difficult cases can be dealt with by not offering a parent the chance to come in, and making appropriate excuses. A more widespread approach is to welcome the parent into an alternative class. This latter technique soon reveals whether there is a genuine interest in helping or if motives are more devious.

Whatever the approach, the teacher has to deal with it and they can, with skill, turn parent involvement to their advantage by developing a client relationship with parents and allowing them to see the many skills of a good, effective teacher at work. In successful relationships the respect of parents for teachers and the job they do will be strengthened with a resulting benefit for the whole school.

Working closely with parents, developing their trust and confidence and handling those who, for whatever reason, present a challenge or who have complaints – either genuine or imagined – all form an important part of the work of those in senior positions in schools and learning this part of the work through day-to-day interaction at classroom level is valuable preparation for career advancement.

There is a word of caution that we would offer any teachers who are involved in working with parents. It is very easy to get sucked into an informal relationship with parents, particularly when working closely with them in the classroom. Although there can be advantages in this, there are potential dangers too and our recommendation is not to let your guard drop and instead to maintain a professional/client relationship at all times. There are many times when informality can turn sour rapidly if an issue arises involving the parent's own child and the need for, perhaps, a firm, objective response by the teacher can be handicapped by previous interaction. Most professionals in other walks of life would offer similar advice. It is very difficult to sustain an ambivalent approach, to retain that necessary professional detachment while being on friendly 'first-name' terms. This can lead a teacher to accusations of being remote and unfriendly, but the long term benefits may be well worth these labels.

Governors in classrooms

Like so many things in education, the role of governors and the way they are perceived have changed in recent years and they are now recognised as forming an important part of the strategic management structure of a school. No longer are governors the remote people who turned up for sports day or concerts, sat in the front row and perhaps said a few words of encouragement at the end in a speech to parents.

Nowadays, Governing Bodies have a formidable list of legal responsibilities and decisions that they are accountable for. It follows that teachers are going to have more involvement with their work and come into contact with them more regularly. The relationships that are built can be of advantage both to the school and also to the individual teacher from a career perspective.

All schools are required to have elected staff governors. Some ambitious teachers see this as an opportunity both to raise their profile with governors and senior management and also, more importantly, as a way of becoming familiar with the range of strategic actions that the governors routinely undertake. It perhaps should go without saying that taking on the role of staff-governor should not be seen as a chance to ingratiate yourself with the governors, but should be a sensible, pragmatic step on the career ladder.

If, as a teacher, you choose not to be formally involved in this way, there should still be plenty of chances to become involved and to demonstrate your expertise in a way that is positively helpful to governors. Some of these are listed below:

- Welcome governors into your classroom (either as volunteer helpers or to allow them to observe a lesson). Be happy to demonstrate your expertise and don't view their presence with suspicion. Note that governors should, and must, attend as lay observers for their own information and are not inspectors or there to comment critically on what happens. Most schools will have a Governor Visits Policy that sets out protocols.

- If you have responsibility for a curriculum area, it is possible that there is also a named governor who has the job of reporting back to the main body on developments and progress in this subject. Be willing to meet this governor routinely and inform them of what is happening. Be prepared to discuss both successes and challenges and try to enlist their support where necessary.

- There may be an opportunity for you to make a presentation to the Governing Body on any particular expertise or responsibility you have. Although some may consider this a daunting prospect, the experience gained will be invaluable.

- Take the trouble to read the minutes of Governing Body meetings when they are published. Apart from keeping you informed about developments affecting the school, you will also gain an insight into the way a strategic body works.

- It is becoming increasingly common for Deputy Heads to be invited routinely to governors' meetings, even if they are not elected governors. This seems sensible if they are to learn the job of Headteacher and see how the dynamics of running a school work in practice.

Schools also have a number of elected parent-governors. As with parent helpers, which we discussed earlier, relationships can be ambiguous. Once again it sometimes happens that parents seek to become governors for the wrong reasons (e.g. hoping to influence actions in relation to their own child), but mostly they are well intentioned and work hard for the benefit of all in the school. What we said in relation to parent helpers and the need to retain a professional distance applies equally, we argue, to governors.

Non-classroom-based support staff

Once you start working in a school you will rapidly come to realise how many people work 'behind the scenes' to keep things going (cleaning and maintenance staff, office staff, meals staff). Working co-operatively with all of these is an essential part of being the consummate professional we advocate you aspire to be; building respect and becoming a recognised leader whom others will turn to for advice and support. There is no room for overlooking the essentially team-based nature of schools and adopting a superior, patronising or dismissive attitude to their efforts. You may have a professional qualification and be among the highest paid employees in the school but that does not provide an excuse for belittling the work of others or for failing to recognise and acknowledge their contribution. It's not just about being liked or showing due courtesy to other workers; moving up the career ladder towards leadership requires a sound understanding of the roles, responsibilities and importance of everyone working in the school and respecting their contribution and the nature of the interdependency that keeps things running smoothly.

Other adults in school

The nature of Primary education means that teachers at all levels of seniority will, in the course of their professional work, have to meet and work with a variety of adults. These can include:

- Education psychologists
- Behaviour consultants
- Local Authority advisers and subject specialists
- Ofsted Inspectors and HMI
- Trainee teachers and their tutors
- Sales representatives
- Visiting speakers and groups (Police, Fire Service, School Nurse, authors).

Each of these visitors will, of course, have a different agenda and will work in a specific way. Their view of the school and their perception of you as an individual will inevitably be coloured by the way you respond to their questions, advice or needs; by the degree of helpfulness you display; and by the extent of the relevant knowledge and expertise you put at their disposal. It is useful when considering how you might work with this range of people to think back to the reference we made in Chapter 2 to developing a professional mantle. If you are professional, measured and objective in your dealings with visitors to the school, and if you maintain an appropriate professional distance in your relationships, being seen as someone who is knowledgeable, informed, open and helpful, you stand a good chance of developing an aura of respect, which will serve to enhance your professional credibility both with your colleagues and with outsiders. Once acquired, you can develop this and carry it with you into future roles as a tool for developing your career.

Developing an 'image'

It's easy to fall into the trap of cynicism when thinking about the idea of 'image'. Image without substance is useless and others will rapidly see through the charade. The image or mantle you adopt has the necessity to develop and evolve in parallel with your skills, expertise and experience. Anything else will leave you open to discovery and ridicule as your mantle falls away to reveal a professional nakedness beneath.

As your career develops, decide what sort of professional you want to be, how you want to be seen by others, and the extent to which you want informality to enter your relationships with colleagues, parents, governors and visitors. This decision will be determined by your own personality and character and will be influenced by your self-confidence, and is something only you can decide upon.

Summary and key actions

- As a classteacher you have overall responsibility for all adults working in your classroom. Make sure you know what they are doing, that you involve them in any planning and that you know what can be expected of them.

- Governors have an important role in the strategic running of schools. Seek ways of working co-operatively with them and remember their lay status and what they can and can't do.

- You may wish to become involved as a governor by seeking election. As a Deputy you should expect to attend meetings as a participant observer.

- Relationships with parent helpers can be difficult. Maintain a professional distance and avoid too much informality.

- Earn the respect of other visitors to the school by co-operating, responding to advice or helping to meet their specific needs.

- Never underestimate or belittle the work of non-class-based school employees. Their contributions to the team are essential and invaluable.

9

A career in the classroom

To lead or not to lead

It is often said that the best teachers usually end up moving from the classroom to become managers and administrators, involved in little if any teaching at all. It is a matter of concern and regret that so many able classroom practitioners feel almost obliged to aspire to these posts, despite their success and love of teaching, because, perhaps, of the perception by others that a full-time career in the classroom in some way represents a lack of advancement or, worse, is a deficit career model of teaching. It is true also that financial rewards for choosing to stay in the classroom have lagged behind those for taking on leadership roles and this may be a sad reflection on the way teaching is viewed.

This chapter focuses on ways of building a career as a full-time teacher and spending most, if not all, of your time in the classroom if that is where your interest lies. We recognise that not everyone who chooses a career in teaching can become a leader, nor that they necessarily want to take this route. There is much to recommend taking the decision to stay in the classroom, not least the fact that you will not find yourself torn between two major roles (being class-teacher and whole-school leader simultaneously). Ultimately, the individual needs to be honest with themself and make a conscious decision about where both their aspirations and their aptitudes lie: some excellent practitioners are not inclined, or indeed suited, to manage other adults, while others are better suited to concentrate on developing their teaching careers in school management where they can influence and contribute strategically to a school.

Of course, teachers are principally trained to teach, not to be personnel and business managers, and this reality is sometimes overlooked both by the blindly ambitious, some of whom, it has to be said, end up being promoted beyond their natural ability. This chapter looks at the merits of developing a rewarding career in the classroom while honing skills and developing sustained expertise in doing the job for which schools exist. Here, we suggest that achieving a satisfactory and rewarding career in the classroom is to do with:

- becoming a flexible, reflective and reflexive exemplar teacher;

- becoming recognised as an expert in a specialist subject (music or PE);

- identifying the opportunities for professional fulfillment through variety, training, teaching by example and reaping the financial rewards that are possible;

- acquiring a reputation as a solid and respectable figure who really makes a difference to pupils' lives and is remembered for this special quality;

- achieving the respect of colleagues as an effective professional who delivers results and can be relied upon.

Much of what we have said earlier about being a professional and how to work smartly applies equally to career teaching in the classroom, so need not be repeated. Moreover, the strategies we have already suggested (e.g. designing your professional 'mantle', having a suitable work/life balance, protecting yourself) is no less pertinent here and will serve you well whatever career path you choose to take in teaching. However, for those who are keen to sustain and develop themselves over many years in the role of classroom practitioner, there are more avenues to pursue, such as mentoring, moving on to the Upper Pay Scale (UPS) and, for the really committed, achieving Leading Teacher Status, as an expert consultant in one or more subject areas.

We said in Chapter 3 that all Primary teachers are expected to assume some kind of whole-school responsibility, following their induction year, usually for a National Curriculum subject area. This is rarely remunerated on top of a teacher's main grade salary. We also pointed out that there are further roles that are frequently managed by classroom teachers and it is among some of these that there is perhaps the greatest opportunity to make a contribution to the development of the school as a whole while remaining first and foremost a teacher.

Additional roles

There are many additional roles that can add variety and play to a teacher's particular strengths to the mutual benefit of the individual and the school: Educational Visits Co-ordinator (EVC), mentor for trainee teachers, organising the school council, recycling club leader, and so on. With new revisions to Teachers' Pay and Conditions implemented from September 2014, all schools now have greater flexibility over their arrangements for rewarding high performance financially. As well as striving for good results, part of a teacher's performance is about their overall effectiveness in contributing to the work of the school. As well as having an area of curriculum responsibility, there are opportunities for committed career teachers to develop additional facets of a school's work and to be recognised for this. While all teachers will nod to the ambiguous compliment that teaching is principally a 'vocation', we would also argue that being remunerated for additional commitment is still a good incentive to perform well – and that this should be no less true in teaching than it is in other caring professions. An advantage of taking on extra responsibility while remaining principally a classteacher, rather than simply climbing the leadership ladder, is the possibility it gives for individuals to develop their own interests (whether sporting, artistic, musical) for the good of the school community as a whole as well as offering useful building blocks in a CV should, at some point, a leadership post become the aim. Culturally, too, classroom teachers who do good things for the school community as a whole tend to earn and enjoy the respect of all of the children, their parents and colleagues. We discussed earlier the relative merits of becoming an acknowledged expert in a particular subject and this is certainly a way in which the 'dedicated' teacher can remain in the classroom while making a significant impact on the success of the school as a whole.

Salary progression and the Upper Pay Scale

Since September 2014, the arrangements for teachers' remuneration have been changed considerably. Now, teachers no longer automatically progress through Points 1 to 6, unless able to demonstrate that they meet a set of demanding nationally applied competencies for teachers ('The Standards' as they are called). Similarly, progression onto the Upper Pay Scale (UPS Points 1–3) has understandably been made more rigorous as well, meaning that it is possible for a teacher to 'get stuck' at any pay point if their performance is not judged by the Headteacher to meet the published criteria (which can also be set according to a school's own preferences) for the next pay point on the scale. Even more radical compared with traditional arrangements is the option to move a teacher 'back' on the pay scale if their performance is judged to have deteriorated since their last appraisal. While this is likely to be rare, presumably applying to the tiny minority of teachers who become the subject of competency proceedings, it does change the stereotypical view that teaching is an easy option if one wishes to progress and earn the best money, since this is, in effect, performance related pay (payment by results) rather than payment by experience, which was hitherto the case for teachers in Maintained Schools. This upheaval of traditional pay arrangements is made even more radical, since it is now possible for a Deputy Head paid on the separate leadership scale to earn more than their Headteacher! How can this be? Under the new arrangements a very experienced Deputy at the top of their institutional pay range could be earning more than a new Headteacher in their school who is appointed at the bottom of their stated pay range on the Leadership Scale. Since 'spot' ranges have now been abolished for members of a school's Leadership Group, governing bodies in effect have *carte blanche*, within very loose parameters, to pay what they choose, as well as to offer both more and less than the traditional rules imposed on them. All of this is to illustrate the fact that incremental pay 'slippage' is now a real possibility for teachers, while the opportunities for capable and ambitious classroom practitioners have never been better; for example, it is now permissible under the new arrangements for a 'superstar' teacher on MPS 1 during their NQT year to be propelled onto the Upper Pay Scale without any of the intervening five salary points having to be earned first. The implications for staffroom morale and internal disputes are far-reaching, but it cannot be ignored that the landscape of teachers' remuneration is changing beyond recognition from what the current generation has come to expect. However, for the ambitious teacher wishing to stay in the classroom, this opens up new possibilities for financial rewards previously considered the preserve of Assistant and Deputy Heads, and their Headteachers. Now more than ever, all teachers should consult their school's pay policy to know where they stand in all eventualities.

Leading Practitioner status

For a number of years the Government has been keen to encourage and make it possible for capable classroom teachers to continue to do what they do best (i.e. teach) by remaining in the classroom and offering financial incentives to do so. Until recently, the route that it was possible to take was by becoming an Advanced Skills Teacher (AST).

Since 2013, the designation of AST has changed to Leading Practitioner (LP) (sometimes referred to as holding Leading Teacher Status). The role is essentially the same. This involves the teacher undergoing additional in-service training and a series of competency tests as part of the selection process, managed in Maintained Schools by the Local Authority. The teacher is also required to be supported by their employing Headteacher and, once accredited, is paid on a separate and higher pay scale than Main Professional Scale teachers. In fact, it has been possible for Lead Practitioners to earn more than some Headteachers, certainly those in areas of high deprivation such as Inner London where funding, and therefore salaries, are often considerably higher than in other parts of the country. As a part of their work, the teacher is expected to model outstanding teaching to their colleagues, through demonstration and team teaching, as well as to undertake outreach work in other schools in the same 'cluster'. Often, the higher salary earned is offset by the employing school providing professional development training for other schools at a cost, paid to the base school.

Although there is a widespread misconception that only schools that have been accredited as National Teaching Schools can employ LPs, this is not the case; any Maintained School or Academy can appoint teachers to these posts and there is considerable scope for 'the relevant body' (usually the employing Governing Body) to remunerate LPs within a stated pay range, often considerably above what the highest classroom teacher is paid.

The introduction of more highly rewarded routes for teachers to stay in the classroom and to disseminate their exemplary practice has undoubtedly acted as a positive incentive for those whose principal vocational aim from the beginning was, and continues to be, to teach, rather than to become a manager or administrator. Our advice would be that such practitioners give serious consideration to these growing opportunities as a genuine alternative for ambitious individuals who do not see themselves as a Deputy or Headteacher. Provided they can earn the professional respect of their colleagues by being credibly and consistently outstanding teachers, and can handle the potential for professional envy from others, being an AST/LP can offer a sustainable professional route for those who are able to meet the demanding standards required.

Being an 'exemplar' teacher

While there is not an absolute consensus about what being 'exemplary' in one's work as a teacher involves, there is little doubt that all of the ideal characteristics described in Chapter 2 apply, whether you are a teacher starting out or an experienced practitioner with years of experience behind you. However, it may be argued that being 'exemplary' as a novice teacher looks somewhat different from being exemplary as an 'expert' teacher. In a way, the term 'expert' conveys the kind of professional wisdom, coupled with experience, that only the years can bring, which goes beyond the level of competency that could ever reasonably be expected of an NQT. Many effective teachers simply acquire these qualities as if by a process of osmosis, that is unconsciously, just as a teacher who is weak will slip through the years, unless they are coached into becoming effective, by repeating the same errors or displaying the same shortcomings year after year. This last possibility is a sobering thought but is, unfortunately, a reality for a minority who really should have considered an alternative career. So, what then is the magic formula for becoming an exemplary teacher and sustaining this role? We suggest the following key principles:

- a moderate and thoughtful approach to the needs of every child in the class;
- consistency in dealing with all pastoral matters, parental concerns or complaints;
- a collegial (i.e. mutually supportive) attitude towards working with others, whether they are 'junior' or 'senior' to your own position in the school;
- an intelligent understanding of the learning process, how planning supports this, and how to make provision for children as individuals;
- professional behaviour and all that it implies: being punctual, dressed appropriately, keeping up-to-date with areas of responsibility, being moderate in tone, high in expectations of self as well as of others, tolerant but clear in values and resilient to attempts at bullying.

This list could go on of course, but the point is a serious one: exemplar teachers are consistent in demonstrating the whole range of professional attributes that are contained in the National Standards for Teachers as well as being balanced, thoughtful professionals who are positive about children and pleasant to work with as a part of the school team. We are not suggesting that such teachers must be able to teach outstanding lessons every time they walk into the classroom, or that they cannot make mistakes on occasion in their approach. Rather, we are arguing that exemplar teachers display their competency and self-control most of the time, such that they are taken seriously by pupils, parents and colleagues alike. This does not mean having to be 'liked' all of the time, but it does mean being seen as being professionally solid and sustaining this capability. This brings us next to the nature of professional reputation.

Professional reputation

The reputation we gain through our work is another nebulous idea, yet everybody knows about it and everybody, to a greater or lesser extent, has one. For teachers, the old cliché that often denotes a teacher with a good reputation is that they are 'firm but fair'. This holds true since it distils two realities about being a competent practitioner that go hand in hand: you cannot teach amid chaos and, therefore, there must be order and adult-led structure for children to learn; and you cannot successfully engage with young people if you are fickle, show favouritism or hand out punishments in an unjust, indiscriminate or immoderate manner. The time when children could be subjugated to the teacher's unshakable authority has long since passed and we now live in a more humane era where justice and respect are the qualities that are expected of those who exercise authority over others, and this is very true in modern teaching. More than this, teachers have to deal with occasionally sensationalised assertions, often promoted through the media, that teachers may not raise their voice to chastise a child, cannot confiscate possessions or, most heinous of crimes, cannot 'touch' their pupils without crossing professional boundaries, thereby ignoring the principles of safeguarding. This last myth should never be taken lightly however: just as schools and teachers have a duty of care to ensure the safety and well-being of all children, teachers themselves need to be vigilant so that their actions never give rise to a cause for concern by others or, much worse, lead to misinterpreted motives. We make this clear for NQTs in Chapter 2 and, provided people are sensible, a congratulatory shake of the hand or an encouraging pat on the shoulder is unlikely to attract criticism. The difference between 'safe' touching and its 'unsafe' antithesis is well known to teachers at all stages in their career and need not be further explained in the context of this book. However, exercising appropriate professional boundaries is a prominent feature of any expert teacher's behaviour.

In fact, experience shows that exemplar teachers, after perhaps an early overly assertive tendency in the youth of their careers, rarely have to shout, take serious punitive action or restrain pupils in the classroom: the equation that a noisy teacher equals a noisy class really does bear out since exemplar teachers do not 'model', and therefore encourage, such deficit behaviour. Instead, exemplar teachers use their considerable experience by learning what works, and what does not, using what is called in educational theory reflective practice, which leads to positive transformation through reflexive (change) practices, giving further rise to a growing professionalism that continues throughout the whole of a teacher's career. As we said at the beginning of this chapter, the real irony is that such teachers often feel compelled to climb the promotional ladder, often taking them out of the classroom, but where they perform best. It does not, though, necessarily follow that an exemplar teacher will have the temperament to become fulfilled as a Deputy or as a Headteacher, with their increasingly strategic roles, and some talented individuals do best if they put all their efforts into giving their all to the job of teaching, which was their first vocational choice.

Grasping opportunity and taking stock

If we accept the premise of this chapter that it is entirely reasonable to develop and sustain a fulfilling career in the classroom, without necessarily aspiring to a school leadership post, then it is a good idea to consider what opportunities will lead to the professional fulfilment you wish for and how to plan a suitable pathway to achieve this. Career satisfaction comes in a number of forms depending on individual preference and personality. There is, though, a set of universal conditions that will apply to all teachers who wish to develop their careers in the classroom:

- They will need to experience variety over time – both in the year group taught and the school setting.

- They will inevitably need to have an opportunity to attend regular training to keep abreast with developments in the National Curriculum and the new initiatives teachers perennially face, both local and national.

- They will need to carve out an area in school where they are the acknowledged 'expert' (perhaps as a co-ordinator) to whom others will go for advice and support.

- They will need to secure and sustain professional credibility among peers, pupils and the wider school community as we suggest above.

It is rare for any teacher to experience professional fulfilment if they find themselves stuck in a single year group for years on end. Headteachers usually aim to spread staff talent around and, even where one of the outstanding teachers is placed, say in Year 6, it is reasonable to expect that these teachers will have an opportunity to broaden their teaching experience within and between each Key Stage over time. On the other hand, teaching in Nursery, Reception and Year 6 have arguably become Primary specialisms in their own right, such is the specific pedagogical knowledge required, for example, to teach in the Early Years. Similarly, the high-stake nature of SATs tests in England and Wales often means that it is the teachers judged to be strongest who are deployed in Year 2 and, in particular, Year 6. This is now especially the case since the recent changes to the Ofsted inspection framework mean that schools are judged much more rigorously on the rates of progress made from individuals' starting points in EYFS, KS1 and KS2, rather than simply children's summative attainment in Year 2 and Year 6 as was previously the case. In smaller schools with fewer staff, it is possible for an effective teacher to find themselves getting stuck in a key year-group leading to the possibility of becoming stale, unstimulated or simply burnt out. This is to be avoided unless an individual has a passion for a given age group and, even where they do, Headteachers will want to feel reassured that the teacher is keeping up-to-date and is not becoming too set in their ways.

Our advice would be that two to three years in any year-group gives the optimum balance between avoiding having to chop and change too much, while having the opportunity to broaden one's experience and sustain a professional 'edge' by being stimulated and rewarded in equal measure. One frustration experienced by many teachers who begin as late entrants, perhaps in their mid to late thirties, is that they find the number of years it takes to build their careers through the various stages precludes their obtaining a significant leadership post, should they aspire to it, once they reach their late forties. This is an uncomfortable truth in spite of the employment legislation prohibiting ageism and, in its way, is understandable. All of this points to the importance of planning key phases of your teaching career as a 'long game' by sketching out key moves which – if this is what you wish – you accomplish in order to make the next step happen; this has been the main purpose of this book. Whether your ambitions lie in the strategic management of the school as a whole or in becoming an expert practitioner based in the classroom, it is vital from the beginning of your career to look forward and to plan, however speculatively and loosely, so that you control your professional pathway to lead you where you want to be within the time you have to achieve these ambitions.

Summary and action

Contrary to the perception by some, the classroom offers a viable and fulfilling career for those who wish to focus on teaching long term, rather than becoming school leaders and administrators. Not all effective classroom teachers are temperamentally suited to becoming Deputies or Heads. There are now a number of career options that provide financial reward as well as vocational satisfaction to those committed to a career in the classroom. Leading Teacher Status offers challenge and fulfilment in equal measure for teachers who are able to develop and sustain themselves as experts in the classroom. Earning a solid professional reputation is key to becoming an exemplar practitioner and will lead to recognition from others in aspiring to the Upper Pay Scale and/or acquiring Leading Teacher Status. To sustain a long and healthy career in the classroom teachers should grasp opportunities for further training and actively seek variety in teaching as many year-groups as possible. From the outset of your career:

• Form an overall plan-of-action for career development, taking into account the age at which you become a teacher – plan key milestones: where do you want to be aged 30? What do you hope to have achieved by age 40? If you aspire to Deputy Headship, by what age do you need to be making this a reality, and so on?

• Be informed about Teachers' Pay and Conditions, the pay scales on the Main Pay Spine for classroom teachers, the Upper Pay Spine and for Leading Teacher Status. Remember to consult these often as there are frequent changes resulting from the annual review by the School Teachers' Review Board (STRB).

10

Deputy Head

The greatest challenge?

Later in this book, in the chapter on making applications, we make the point that Deputy Headship is considered by some to be the most difficult and challenging job in a Primary School. This may be thought to be a strange assertion given that the post is effectively that of second in relation to the role of Headteacher, who bears ultimate responsibility for the running of the school, but we have no doubt that doing the job properly requires a special combination of skills, experience and personal characteristics, including stamina and resilience, which, it has to be said, some teachers do not possess. Further, the need to maintain a balance in relationships between leadership and the rest of the staff is far from easy for many. The situation is further complicated by the fact that in many Primary Schools, particularly the smaller ones, the Deputy can find themselves with a heavy teaching load and possibly even full-time class responsibility.

It follows from this argument that a career move of this sort should not be undertaken lightly and that if you are considering moving to Deputy Headship you should be fully acquainted with the demands of the role and match these with your own qualities. To fail to do so risks leaving you vulnerable to working under pressures that may prove too much for you over time with the consequences of unhappiness, personal stress and even competency issues in extreme cases. The role of Deputy Headteacher in any school has at its heart the moral and professional imperative to provide the best possible education for all of the school's pupils: without this commitment, and the ability to have a major strategic impact on achievement and standards, a Deputy Headteacher's place in the school is an ineffectual one.

An additional feature that can contribute to this situation is the fact that a move to Deputy Headship represents in some respects a passing of a 'point of no return' on the career ladder. Unless you have been through the intermediate stage of Assistant Head, you will be moving from Main Scale, or the Upper Pay Scale, to the Leadership Scale with all that implies in respect of changes to conditions of service and expectations, and you will be making a statement about your intention to move towards becoming a school leader. The implication of seeking to make this move is that you judge yourself, and have been judged by others, to have clear potential to take on the running of a school and this, like moving to any executive position, is a rite of passage that, ideally, should really be a one way street. Of course it's always possible to return to Main Scale teaching if the work as a Deputy doesn't suit or work out, though not perhaps in the same school. However, in the context of career development this can only be seen as a retrograde step from which it might prove difficult or impossible to recover, and one that, for reasons of personal pride and job satisfaction, most would rather avoid.

When to apply

Before taking a decision to begin to apply for Deputy posts, therefore, we recommend that you carry out a self-appraisal to judge how successful you have been in middle-management in making a positive impact, how you have coped with an increased workload and, more importantly, how much you have enjoyed and felt comfortable with the associated responsibility. Take into account, also, the views and opinions of others, listen to what they say, both informally and in the course of performance management meetings. These days the post of Deputy involves more than being a highly paid classteacher who looks after the school on the odd days when the Head is out. Although this may once have been the case, there is now an expectation from all quarters for the Deputy to become involved in strategic leadership and decision-making at every level within the school and to have a significant influence and impact on its development and success.

It is true also that the notion of the 'career Deputy' is fast disappearing and the post is now seen widely as a preparation or as an 'apprenticeship' for Headship. It may be argued, therefore, that if you have no wish ultimately to become a Headteacher and to run your own school, you should not think of applying for Deputy Headship. This may sound like harsh advice, but the reality is that good quality Headteachers need to have worked as Deputies and learned about the intricacies of school management in this way. If the route is blocked by those who don't have such aspirations, the supply of good leaders begins to dwindle and problems are stored up for the future.

Learning the craft

Taking a more positive view and assuming that you have successfully gained a Deputy Headship, how can this post be best managed to your advantage in preparation for the next, and perhaps definitive, career move?

The working relationship with the Headteacher is, we suggest, key to success in the role. Ideally, there needs to be a matching of complementary skills and a shared idea of how the school can progress. A clash of philosophies is, to say the least, unhelpful. A Headteacher should feel confidently able to delegate major tasks to the Deputy and, in many respects, consider them almost as an equal in the running of the school. The Deputy will learn by doing and by seeing at close quarters the Head engaged in a range of activities associated with leadership. Involvement in governors' meetings, performance management, budget setting and staff appointments should be routine and there should be no professional secrets between the two senior leaders. The best Head/Deputy relationships thrive on shared values, mutual respect and trust, as well as regular and effective communication. If any of these is lacking things will not work out for the best and the relationship will founder. In short, it helps greatly if you actually like each other as people, feel able to work together and have common goals. Although it is not always entirely practical to do so, it is advisable as far as possible to make a judgment about the likely success of this working relationship when you are at the application stage. Asking questions of the Headteacher, and maybe even the departing Deputy if possible, as well as looking at school policies and practices, will give you some insight into the way senior management in a particular school works and allow you to gauge whether it conforms to your expectations and to decide whether you will fit in. In all probability, the Headteacher will be forming similar judgments about your suitability so that a potential mismatch becomes less likely. The governors too will have a view of what sort of person they would like to appoint. As with other applications for posts in schools, it is important not to jump at opportunities without weighing up the relative merits and disadvantages and considering whether it is really what you want and whether this really is the job for you. A spell as Deputy to a Headteacher who does not support you, delegate to you or take you into their confidence is of minimal help in your career aspirations and can lead to frustration and disillusionment.

It is important to recognise that the Deputy Head is in a strong position to influence and lead school developments. It is not, or should not be, a passive role. A good Head will recognise this and will allow you professional freedom, welcome ideas and initiatives and create an atmosphere of innovation in which the Deputy is able to flourish and develop their strengths. While in the early days a new Deputy should expect and receive a great deal of guidance and support, one who is always waiting to be told what to do, deferring to others, or unwilling to act without instruction will not be doing justice to the role. You must expect to be proactive rather than reactive and this should be encouraged and applauded by the Headteacher and others.

Being in this position means that your judgment and discretion will be tested on many occasions. Faced with a challenging situation or problem, can you make an appropriate decision? Are you decisive or do you dither and defer to others, or worse still, get on the phone to the Head, who may be at a meeting or at home ill, to ask what to do?

Targets for career development as a Deputy

Once appointed as a Deputy, you should seek every opportunity to broaden your experience and you should expect to be involved regularly in the following:

- Governors' meetings and committees. Attend and contribute to the discussions. Not necessarily as an elected governor but as an observer in your own right.
- Shortlisting, interviewing and appointments of staff.
- Meetings with external agents – 'Challenge Partners', LA Advisers and, of course, Ofsted.
- Observation and performance management of teaching staff and appraisal of support staff.
- Budget planning.
- Staff disciplinary issues.
- Pastoral issues involving pupils.
- Meetings with parents.
- Strategic planning – resourcing, curriculum, staff allocation.
- Target setting.
- Drafting of the School Improvement Plan and other key documents.

Involvement with all of the above has a number of advantages, not only to you from a career development standpoint, but also to the school and your leadership colleagues. Some of these benefits may not be immediately apparent but the job will give you many rewards:

- You gain first-hand experience of all aspects of the Headteacher's role in running the school.
- You become familiar with the strategic parts of school management.
- You are seen by your colleagues, governors and parents to be a key member of the leadership team, making an active contribution to the running and development of the school.
- Your presence at meetings – particularly potentially difficult ones – demonstrates support for the Headteacher and builds the co-operative bond in the working partnership.
- Your own confidence is steadily developed.
- The leadership role is shared so that all the burdens of responsibility do not rest on one person.
- In circumstances where the Head is absent from school for any length of time, you are familiar with all areas of school management and are able to take command seamlessly.

It is certainly true that this situation does not pertain in all schools and depends largely on the willingness of the Headteacher to involve the Deputy in this range of tasks and the readiness of the Deputy to become involved. We put it forward here as an ideal to be aspired to and one that will give a Deputy with ambitions for Headship the maximum exposure to beneficial experiences. If you are not presented with the chance to participate in the way we suggest, it may be appropriate for you to raise the matter with the Head who may, perhaps through their own inexperience, not realise that involvement of the Deputy to this extent is possible and desirable.

Other professional development

We have made it clear that there will be great demands placed on you as a Deputy Headteacher and that, particularly in the early stages, you will find the work challenging. Nevertheless we suggest that your period as Deputy is also a time when you should be consolidating your professional knowledge in other ways.

If you have not already done so, you should consider taking further academic or professional qualifications (a Master's degree or NPQH) to give further strength to any future application for Headship. Your ability to do this and the ease with which you are able to take on the extra work will depend on support from your Headteacher and the extent of commitments in school and at home. If you have a heavy teaching role, it may be difficult for the school to arrange for the necessary release, but we would certainly recommend this as a course of action to be considered.

Standing in for the Head

Although the post title implies that the Deputy is there to replace the Head during his or her absence, the reality is that this does not necessarily occur that often and is certainly not normally a major part of the role. It would, after all, be inefficient to pay someone on an enhanced salary scale simply so that they were able to step in as a replacement for someone else as required and to expect them to do nothing else in the meantime to justify the salary.

This does not mean, however, that there will not be times when the deputising role comes to the forefront. There are generally three ways in which this can happen:

- the Headteacher is unable or unwilling to attend a meeting or some similar activity away from the school and asks the Deputy to go instead;
- the Headteacher is out of school for a day or part of a day and leaves the day-to-day running of the school to the Deputy;

- the Headteacher is absent for an unforeseen extended period due to illness and the Deputy is required to take over all aspects of the running of the school.

None of these three possibilities should cause an ambitious Deputy any undue worries or problems. Obviously, a more experienced Deputy will find them less challenging than someone new to the job, but anyone in this position should possess the range of skills and experience necessary to cope well, and indeed welcome the chance to take temporary charge of the school. There are a number of things that you should bear in mind though:

1   If the Head's absence was planned, have you been properly briefed about things that are likely to crop up and how best to deal with them?

2   If you are attending a meeting on behalf of the Head, do you know what is involved, have you seen an agenda and, if any decisions have to be taken, do you understand the implications of different forms of action and what the school's preferred response is?

3   In the event of unplanned or longer term absence, do you take account of school policies when taking decisions? Do you ask yourself, 'what would the Head do in these circumstances?'? In these extended absences it is more likely that you will be required to make decisions and take actions that have longer-term implications. Although you will be expected to act decisively, it would be reasonable to consult others, e.g. the Chairman of Governors, other members of the SMT, or the Head him/herself if available, before taking any actions that have major implications.

Although it is wise, and courteous, to keep the Head informed of actions you have taken during his/her absence, you should avoid being seen to seek advice on everything you do and, having taken decisions, you must stand by them and be prepared to justify them. Your Headteacher should be able to support your decisions fully.

If there is a longer term absence of the Headteacher – say a term or more – then it is normal for the Deputy to be given acting rank to recognise the situation and to enable them to function fully as a leader. Although you would no doubt not wish an extended absence on the Headteacher, there is certainly a great career advantage in serving a period as Acting Headteacher, and it works wonders with your CV to be able to demonstrate that you have run a school for a time.

All things to all (wo)men

Something that Deputies frequently find themselves having to do is to take on responsibilities by default. Although many will have key management responsibilities in their own right, e.g. SENCo, Phase Manager, subject leader, which take up a significant part of their working time, it sometimes happens that other curriculum areas are not being led, perhaps due to staff shortages, and the Deputy is asked to step in. Once more, this is a mixed blessing. Extra work and more demands on time, but a chance to show versatility, enthusiasm and resourcefulness, and to give a lead to the rest of the staff. This sort of thing goes with the job and is something you must come to expect.

It is often said that the Deputy Head should be the best teacher in the school. This can be a tall order and in our view is not a prerequisite of the post. What we would agree with is that the Deputy should be a sound practitioner who follows policies, has good classroom management skills and is able to exemplify good and outstanding teaching. The challenge here, especially in larger schools where the Deputy's teaching timetable may be small, is keeping up-to-date with current practice and retaining familiarity with teaching technique. It can be far too easy to distance yourself from the classroom once you become involved in strategic management and to become out of touch with the day-to-day task of teaching.

The next step

As a serving Deputy, you need to have in mind your next career move. This raises two questions. How long should you plan to stay in post, and will you seek a Headship or the Deputy Headship of a larger school? It's always advisable to have the length of time you plan to stay in a post at the back of your mind. This does not of course have to be binding, but it helps to focus your attention on the future and allows you to avoid getting too comfortable or complacent in your post.

Some Deputies seek a second post in a larger school as a way of building experience and gaining the understanding of a different management style. Financially, there is usually an advantage to this type of move, but this has to be balanced against the expectation that you might feel obliged to stay in this second post for a number of years before seeking to move on to Headship. Your age needs to be taken into consideration here. There's no absolute rule about the best age to take on Headship, but appointing bodies may have their own unspoken view and in that case it's wise not to leave things too late. The other disadvantage of this approach is that you might have in mind applying for a specific Headship in your area, one that you know may be coming up at some stage. Committing to a further period as Deputy somewhere else can hamper this ambition. You should also ask yourself the question, 'Am I seeking a further Deputy Headship to gain experience or because I am lacking in the confidence necessary to run a school myself?'.

Summary and action

- To be an effective Deputy Head is a very challenging job. Be convinced that you have the necessary qualities before applying.
- Deputy Headship is a form of apprenticeship. Use the time to learn the skills of running a school.
- Expect to be heavily involved in all aspects of running the school and to be given freedom to innovate. Be proactive not reactive.
- Be decisive when managing the school in the Head's absence. Seek advice on major issues but avoid the temptation to defer to others on every matter.
- Consider using the time as Deputy for professional development to build your CV in support of any application for Headship.
- Keep up your currency as a teacher. Avoid the risk of distancing yourself from the classroom.
- Think carefully about the length of time ideally you aim to serve as a Deputy and what your subsequent move will be. Are you content to seek Headship or do you want another Deputy Headship in a larger school?

11

Your first Headship

Taking over a school

Like most people, your journey to the 'Big Chair' of Headship will probably be tortuous, frustrating and hard-fought. Although everybody's experience is different, almost all will have to negotiate a number of career obstacles and challenges to get there. Very few people are handed a Headship on a plate and most have to face multiple disappointments before they finally succeed. In this chapter, we consider the significance of this defining career move. We want to be open but positive about the inevitable challenges being a Head will bring, and we talk about the most common scenarios the first-time Headteacher is likely to find awaiting them. Headship is a unique role, at once the most exciting job in the world for those who are suited to it, while at the same time just possibly among the more stressful occupations it is possible to have. We talk about how to make a positive impact, common pitfalls to avoid and how to deal with the level of responsibility and the stress this can invoke. Above all, we want to make it clear that Headship is not for everyone and that it is possible to build a rewarding career in teaching that sustains you throughout your working life without necessarily having to aspire to school leadership.

If you are still reading this chapter, you must at least be mildly interested in pursuing Headship as a possibility. Perhaps you are already looking at posts as an experienced Deputy or you are thinking well ahead about what your career might hold for you later on. Either way, we want to pass on our experience of Headship in Primary Schools, not so much as an example of how to do it, but as a means of encouraging you to develop a realistic impression of what is involved in it. Of course, there is no single template for a successful Headteacher, but there are certain characteristics that will allow the individual to handle Headship more confidently once they are in post and, for the first time in their careers, find that they are in charge of their own school.

This is the remarkable thing about being Headteacher. You are the 'boss' with no line-manager to report to. Admittedly there is a Governing Body to whom you are accountable and that can collectively direct the Headteacher, within certain strategic limits. Some people mistakenly think the school's Chair of Governors is line-manager to the Head. This is not the case and the Chair has no more power than any other governor, other than being able to exercise a delegated authority of 'Chair's Action' in certain circumstances.

The applications and selection processes – both general and specifically for senior posts such as Headship – are discussed in Chapters 12 and 13. Here, we talk about what your first Headship will likely bring, and how to steer a steady path through the early stages of doing the job.

You have nervously arrived at your new school on your first day (and you will be nervous despite any front that you might affect). You walk into the building exchanging pleasantries, and that's it, you are the Headteacher!

Unless you have been appointed from within the school, having previously been the Deputy, it is likely that you will not know the names of most, if any, of the staff, you won't be acquainted with the routines, you won't know where things are, and, when they start curiously trying to find out about their new Headteacher, you won't know any of the children's names either. Coming from the familiarity and relative 'safety' of your old school, the feeling of not knowing anything about anything is, for many, unsettling.

One of the biggest anxieties often experienced by new Heads, once they've arrived on their first day, is what will happen next. The reality is that nothing usually does happen! You might be the one ultimately responsible and in charge, but everybody else will know what they are doing and will just go about their business as usual and the school will simply run as it always does. This can be disconcerting, but do make the most of this honeymoon period since it will eventually give way in a day or two to reveal the many new and unfamiliar tasks and challenges facing you and with everybody suddenly wanting a piece of you and answers to innumerable questions. This can be overwhelming at first and you need to equip yourself with strategies to cope. Everyone experiences this sudden surge of activity and the trick is to anticipate it. The most common onset of multiple demands usually comes from members of your staff, many of whom may have come to rely on your predecessor for guidance and direction (e.g. it looks like rain, should we have indoor break time today?). Faced with this, it is wise simply to ask what would normally happen. The answer is usually already suspected by the colleague asking, but seeking your reassurance that they can continue just as before, at least for the time being. This is usually all it takes to keep the school going as it customarily does.

What are you taking on?

No two Headships are alike, such are the variations between schools. There are, however, common features. You will have the day-to-day responsibility for the management and smooth running of the school as well as the strategic responsibility for standards in all year-groups, the welfare and control of staff, for managing the school budget and for forming and realising what is usually called your 'vision' for the further improvement of the school. The Governing Body of the school vests a wide range of delegated responsibilities in the Headteacher and it is important to realise that this authority is, in effect, a finite one, with no prerogative for the governors to line-manage the Headteacher. Despite the considerable power you will wield you will still be accountable for your professional actions and capability to the governors as a collective body and, by extension, the regulatory body under which the school operates, for example the Local Authority, Trust or Foundation.

Within the school community, the role of the HT is all encompassing. For those with the ambition, the stamina and temperament, there's no other job like it. You may find that you are taking over from an established and respected figurehead and this is a sobering thought. Alternatively there may have been a long *inter-regnum* with a Deputy or temporary Head running things. Whatever the circumstances there will be a period of settling-in that will include all or some of the following experiences:

- the feeling that you have started all over again and are experiencing a drop in professional confidence;

- the perception that others are trying you out and testing your judgment and ability;

- being frequently compared to your predecessor – this can have positive or negative connotations;

- a sense of isolation when it dawns on you that your office is where any big issue will end up;

- bereavement: missing your old school and former colleagues who have become friends.

There are advantages to taking over a school that has experienced some problems or is in a shabby state, since you can be more confident that whatever you do to improve matters will be seen in a positive light. It is much harder to take over a school that is described by Ofsted as 'outstanding', since any changes you make must demonstrate that you can maintain its reputation and perceived excellence. In an outstanding school, there is only one possible direction in which to travel! This raises the question: do you have clear ideas about how you want to develop the school or are you just keeping it warm as a 'caretaker Head' for your own successor?

Whatever the circumstances, your first appointment as Headteacher is guaranteed to offer some of the biggest challenges of your professional life. Initially, these mainly concern how you develop your leadership style, and use this to good effect: how you establish yourself as a credible authority figure in the eyes of the school's community; how you build trust among your colleagues; how you deal with problems and issues that crop up from time to time; and how you go about consulting the key 'stakeholders' before making informed policy decisions – in summary, how you actually 'manage' your new school.

Developing your leadership style

There is a whole literature on the subject of management styles and leadership. How you 'style' yourself will largely depend on your approach in earlier management posts. You will already have been a middle-manager and senior leader in a school and will have developed your approach and be well known for it. The great thing about taking on any post in a new setting is the opportunity it gives for you to re-style yourself to some extent. If you have made any errors along the way (and we all have), you will now have the chance in your new environment to avoid making the same mistake twice. This is easier said than done, of course, and does require a degree of soul-searching and re-living some of those moments you would prefer to forget, and you will need to be honest with yourself, to consider not just your strengths and abilities but also your foibles and faults. As Deputy Headteacher, were you:

- A 'martinet', always bossing others around?
- A 'soft touch', easily manipulated by your colleagues?
- A 'Deputy-for-all-seasons' (everybody's friend)?
- A 'temperamentalist', sometimes upbeat and jaunty, at others touchy and unapproachable?
- A consummate professional with a balanced approach and respected by all?

There are no prizes for guessing which stereotype we would all wish to be. We could go on with these stereotypes of course, and it is usual that we all have a combination of character traits to a greater or lesser extent. But it is your more prominent traits, those that your colleagues recognise you for, that will likely influence the impression you first make as a new Headteacher. Will you be viewed as autocratic or as democratic, or perhaps as something between these extreme positions? As with any promotion, it is much more difficult to adopt a change if you are moving up within the same school, but it is undeniably a wonderful opportunity for you to re-examine yourself and to make a conscious effort to shed some of your less attractive foibles when you move on to somewhere new. Why is this important? As Headteacher, you are the public 'face' of the school. In a sense, you *are* the school and this feeling, as it grows in you, can bring a sense of great pride as well as lead you to take any criticism of the school personally. As you gain in experience, you will learn to develop a special Headteacher's version of your professional mantle, described in Chapter 2, as you experience and deal with the inevitable highs and lows and, ever so gradually, develop an asbestos skin, both for the school's sake and for your own.

The core characteristics that you should aim to demonstrate from your first day as Headteacher are those related to the conventionally sensible ones now helpfully enshrined, or implied, in the National Standards for Teachers. We would advise that you:

- Demonstrate a fair and consistent approach to your dealings with all pupils, their parents/carers and your colleagues.

- Have the interpersonal qualities to consult others, yet have the fortitude, following any consultation, to make an independent decision without flinching or seeking refuge in easy consensus.

- Be prepared to listen fully to others before making a decision. This is especially important where, as is commonplace, you have a dispute or disciplinary matter to deal with.

- Communicate clear high expectations of others but ensure that you, too, espouse these values. For instance, do you expect your colleagues to be on time for meetings, but are often late for appointments yourself? Two examples here will illustrate this point. While it is considered unacceptable for teachers to be late for the weekly staff meeting, some Heads fail to recognise the importance of putting a time limit on meetings, thereby not allowing team members to plan their other commitments and their domestic life. In the worst cases, staff meetings can go on and on until nobody has anything else to say. Another example concerns the formal observation of a teacher's lesson. If the lesson begins straight after lunchtime, it is vital to be in the classroom a few moments beforehand to observe the children coming in and to see the lesson commence.

- Keep an organised diary, meeting all deadlines (for example, the Headteacher's termly report to the Governing Body) and always demonstrate a level of professional reliability that puts you beyond any criticism or reproach.

- Avoid becoming over-familiar with colleagues, some of whom will warm to you because they genuinely like you, while others will be sycophantic in order to try to manipulate you.

- Be prepared to confront the less savoury aspects of being in charge: workplace bullying, aggressive or unreasonable parents, provocative governors, sad events and Ofsted inspection.

- Try to be a role model in your temperament while at work. In other words, greet colleagues, pupils and their parents equitably in the morning, even if you have had an argument at home or feel under pressure due to the way your week is going.

- Remember, always to act in the best interests of your pupils, which, by extension, means the school community as a whole. There is no place for effective Headteachers to become self-interested or partisan.

- Always be on your guard: everything you say or do as a Headteacher will be noticed by everyone whom you encounter. For example, even the friendly parent who has been welcoming from your first day and always has a chat with you at the school gate each morning has the potential to turn on you when they become unhappy about something.

- Learn how to delegate effectively, if you haven't already done so as a Deputy, because, if you don't, you can easily find yourself in a situation whereby you end up doing more than you can handle. Remember, your purpose as Headteacher is to develop your 'vision' for the school's evolution from a strategic perspective. If you become prone to micro-managing everything, you will lose sight of what you hope to achieve. When you delegate a task or function to a colleague, let them carry it out without your interference. They are still accountable to you for carrying out their role to your satisfaction, but managers who keep pestering their team members with questions and requests for frequent updates soon cause resentment from the group and risk losing any loyalty they had hoped to earn.

- Above all, always act and dress as an exemplar professional. It would be hypocritical for the Headteacher to impose a dress code for the staff, and to enforce a school uniform policy strictly, if they turn up for school looking casually dressed or un-groomed.

Building a culture of trust

Many of the maxims outlined above will allow you to build a culture of trust when you take up your Headship. Two things are paramount in addition, though, and should always be present at the back of your mind:

- Always exercise a discreet approach to all matters, especially personal ones. As Headteacher, you will be privy to many staff confidences, both personal and professional. It is essential that those who share their confidences know that you can be trusted with them.

- Never make a promise you cannot keep. There will be many situations in which others will appeal to you for something they want or believe they deserve, and you might be tempted to indulge them, as a way of courting popularity, especially if it is a teacher you are anxious to keep on the staff, and the promise of a promotion or a change of role might influence their decision, but the risks of this approach are great and you should always exercise caution.

Making a positive impact

As soon as you arrive, there will be inevitable speculation about your plans for the school. What will you change, what will you improve, what might you ruin? The speculation will extend to both your 'style', and your personal life, and some will be anxious to find out what implications your arrival will have for them personally and what the effect will be on their role in school. You should anticipate that some staff will pre-empt your actions and may want to get in first by seeking an early meeting with you. Don't be drawn into rushed decisions.

The future of the whole school now rests with you, at least for as long as you stay, so how do you make a positive impact on what you find, whether the school is pristine and popular or ramshackle and struggling? The answer is two-fold. Any immediate changes you make should, ideally, be those that are relatively easy for you to achieve and that will be popular with the vast majority of people. Second, be careful not to be too revolutionary, too quickly. People often feel threatened by change, so pick your changes carefully and wisely so that they are most likely to win plaudits. That is not to say you should avoid being unpopular or taking unpopular decisions if you judge them to be right, but only pick a battle that you know you can win. You cannot hope to make the bigger changes that you probably already see as necessary if you do not have your 'troops' behind you. You need time to work out who your allies are and who might turn out to be an enemy. This does not usually take long since most people rapidly show their true colours and, in reality, this means that, at worse, you will find a small number of defectors who use the departure of your predecessor as a pretext for taking the next step in their own careers elsewhere. This is to be expected and, for the new Headteacher, is a helpful way of creating an opportunity to begin recruiting new people for their team. The resulting influence of such 'new blood' can bring fresh ideas to a school and enliven its culture. It is a natural phenomenon in any organisation that the arrival of a new leader precipitates shifts in staffing, and the advice is not to expect that you will achieve your idealised vision in the short term. Indeed, it is fair to say that it takes a new Head over a year to settle in comfortably, two years to feel more at home, three to turn around a school, and at least five years to make a really long lasting positive impact on standards and facilities. The antithesis is that it takes just a year for an inept Head to ruin a school! Many Heads like to stay in their first Headship for at least the seven years it takes for an entire cohort to go through the school. After this time, some will start to look for that next challenge in school leadership, a bigger school with better financial rewards or, perhaps, the next step in their careers in education moving them beyond school-based work.

Perhaps the best tactic a new Head can adopt is to work out quickly what it is that gives a school its distinctive identity (its ethos) and to nurture and promote these things. It might be that the school is notable for its sporting achievements, or for its musical prowess, its excellence in art or links with overseas schools. Every school has something that sets it apart, and it is wise to reassure the whole community that you will preserve and value the things they treasure even if it is something that you do not feel strongly about. If, for example, the school has a culture of inter-school competition and many after-school clubs, it would be foolhardy to go against this grain. The Headteacher is the school's public face and, politically, will be expected to uphold its traditional values, even if this involves standing on the touchline in the winter to cheer on your football team despite the thought leaving you cold. Be clear: your presence will not be commented on, but your absence will be noted.

This is not to suggest that you content yourself with 'caretaking' everything that you inherited from your predecessor's time. Rather, you need to take control carefully and gently and spend time watching, listening, understanding and evaluating all the new things for which you are now the leader. Only when you have become intimately knowledgeable about the workings of your school, can you confidently start to make subtle changes to its course, if indeed this is necessary, or to change direction completely if this is what needs to be done. Before you seek to change something though, find out why it happens. There may be good reasons that you have not seen and you need to avoid the embarrassment of a change of heart later. In the meantime, the safest approach will be to make a positive impact by making uncontroversial changes that will win universal appreciation: new playground equipment for playtimes, a lick of paint, new cushions and a dishwasher for the tired staffroom, time-limited staff meetings and so on. If you can win some widespread approval for changes that make life more pleasant for everyone in your first few weeks, you can then begin to look forward to a long term campaign to make the school yours, for the benefit of all of your pupils and colleagues. There is no secret to all of this, as long as you stand back, look at the whole scene and take each carefully considered step forwards in your new Headship one day at a time.

Professionalism

As well as being the public face of your school and its community, you will also be the subject of a good deal of scrutiny in the way you conduct yourself. More than anybody else, others will take note of your:

- appearance and dress
- voice and use of language
- attitude towards discipline and the way you deal with it
- manner when put under pressure
- way of dealing with tricky parents
- reliability and time-keeping
- philosophy of teaching and learning.

This can at first feel like being permanently under scrutiny. There are some techniques you can adopt that will help to alleviate this feeling and they are outlined merely as suggestions at the end of this chapter. Therefore, it is important that, when 'on duty', a Headteacher both looks and feels the part and behaves accordingly. In other words, the Head must exude an air of professionalism at all times, whatever the circumstances and however challenging, since this is what everybody will expect. Further, your school will be judged largely by the reputation that you give to it and this realisation, especially for the beginning Headteacher, is a sobering one.

Looking after yourself

If, when you were a classteacher, you came to value your privacy and the ability to become an anonymous member of the public when away from school, you will value your 'escapes' into a private life even more as Headteacher. In our view, the best expressions of professionalism in Headship accommodate both personae – the authoritative, reassuring presence as Head and the free adult with a private life away from the gaze of the school community. This may be one reason, among many others, for not living too close to your place of work and is something you may wish to consider when applying for posts.

The dangers inherent in excessive stress, especially over time, are well known. There is a multitude of measures we can take to reduce stress in order to remain healthy and to be content, and you will be wise to anticipate stress while considering your own personal triggers for it in order to pre-empt a build up. Much of what we said in the second chapter applies here in just the same way, although there is a specific metaphorical 'mantle' you can wear as a new Head that will help to preserve you when you are in Headteacher 'mode'. You should consider:

- The rules you establish about access to your office – do people just walk in or do they knock? Do you indicate that you are engaged if your door is firmly closed and that you may be disturbed if your office door is left ajar?

- Are you addicted to email? This is a burgeoning problem among all kinds of workers and, with the advent of new technology, makes it even harder to switch off from work since it can become a compulsion to check school emails at all times of the day, during the weekend and when you are away on holiday. Some out-of-hours email work will usually be necessary, but the new Head should find a way to control the urge to keep checking and, indeed, avoid feeling the need to check each day during the school holidays. One approach that makes the point that you are not available twenty-four hours a day, is to set the automatic out-of-office reply for the period you wish to be 'off duty'. It is ironic that email, originally vaunted as a boon to administrative efficiency, has largely become the bane of managers' lives – keep email in its box and learn to apply the lid!

• How you signal to others (especially parents) that you are not there to deal with every issue or complaint – do you take over when a parent moans about something at the school gate or do you refer them either to the classteacher in the first instance or other appropriate member of staff (e.g. Key Stage Leader or Deputy Head)?

• Do some people have 'special access' to you whenever they feel like it, meaning that you are constantly interrupted with trivial demands? If you do find yourself being perpetually consulted at the whim of, say, the secretary, do you need to 'train' your colleague so that, when your door is closed, you are not interrupted except for an urgent matter that must involve you?

• How you deal with being put on the spot by an enquiry that 'throws' you. These come from parents and staff members in equal measure. Do you listen, say thank you and inform the enquirer that you will think about it and get back to them, buying valuable time to think?

In all of these contexts it is very easy, even as the Headteacher, to find that you encourage a situation in which you don't feel comfortably in control and in which others are determining your responses and actions. As Head, you might be responsible for the whole school but this does not mean that you have to take personal responsibility for everything, or do everything yourself risking your ability to carry out the more strategic tasks that you will need to attend to in your normal working day. Some Headteachers believe that they must set an example to their staff by working more hours than anybody else. Managers have to manage, but the art of this is in managing others to carry out what needs to be done operationally so that you stand back and take an overview.

Summary and action

Becoming a Headteacher puts you in a powerful position, but can also make you vulnerable. You need to consider carefully and deal thoughtfully with what you are taking on when you assume the role. No two Headships are alike but there is a common set of ideals to which you can aspire and some fundamental principles that you can apply to your new position in order to succeed in the early days of Headship. Consider:

• how you will develop your management style, establishing your position successfully following the transition from your predecessor;

• how you will aim to build a culture of trust among all members of the school community;

- how you will make an initial impact that is a safe bet and will be appealing to everybody in your new school;

- how you will adapt your professional mantle and come to exude a level of professionalism and wisdom that befits the office of Headteacher;

- how you will train yourself to be resilient and look after your own health and emotional well-being.

12

Preparing your application

The principle of making an application for a teaching post is essentially the same for first teaching appointments, for a teacher's second post involving increased responsibility, trying for a Deputy Headship and, ultimately, applying for Headship itself. In short, the application has the singular objective of securing an interview for the post for which you have applied.

In this chapter, we take each of these four types of application in turn – first NQT posts, promotion, Deputy Headship and Headship – and suggest how to approach each kind in order to maximise the chances of winning an interview. However, although it is certainly true that different posts require a different approach, there is also a set of common principles that apply to all posts and that must be mastered if success is to be had in what, after all, is a competitive situation, one in which you will wish to distinguish yourself from all the others in order to be chosen. These universal principles can be summed up as:

- writing style
- grammar and punctuation
- chronology
- experience and impact
- proofreading.

Rather than offer a 'model' application statement by way of illustration, since this can lead to the reproduction of generic and ill-matched applications (see below), we will examine the subtleties of writing applications for different career stages in teaching, giving some solid ideas that will enable you to make the application your own. Finally, we summarise this chapter with some cardinal rules that all applications *should* follow if they are likely to lead to an invitation to interview. First, though, we need to consider the four main types of application and look at each one in turn.

First teaching posts

In a sense, this is the most important application of all, since it will be the one that launches your career in teaching. Surprisingly, perhaps, relatively few applicants really distinguish themselves for the right reasons and most applications are generic in their content as well as being, it must be said, poorly constructed and badly written. In our experience, very few applications for NQT posts are impressive and persuasive. This is a pity, since good beginning teachers often fail to secure their first post, losing a job that they would have won earlier and been happy in had their application been more impressive in the first place. Ironically, the greater emphasis on writing applications as a part of courses of initial teacher training seems to have led to greater genericism among applicants' written statements, making it harder for them to stand out for the right reasons. Some of this has to do with the quality of advice, or lack of it possibly, among the HE providers. Whatever the cause, recruiting Headteachers commonly cite the number of poorly written applications as a problem.

There are two parts to a written application for a first post – the application form and the written statement in support of the application. It is now a requirement by all employers in the public sector that an application form must be submitted rather than the more traditional *curriculum vitae* (CV). This is because of the nature of working with children and other vulnerable people and the fact that a standardised form controls, very precisely, the information that an applicant is required to supply. The most important of these is to do with chronology (i.e. the applicant being required to account for every period in their life since leaving school aged 16 or 18). This is important since 'gaps' in an applicant's past could imply a material fact that the applicant would prefer to hide, for example a period of imprisonment. By requiring a continuous chronology to be stated on the form, the prospective employer controls this agenda and can hold the applicant responsible if any period is not accounted for or, worse, a period is deliberately omitted. Should any applicant fail to disclose their past history honestly, it is likely that employment would be terminated if, and when, the truth emerges, however delayed the discovery might be. This of course, would depend on the nature of the omission, whether or not it was an error or deliberate, and crucially if it had any material bearing on the nature of employment itself. In Independent Schools, however, it is not unusual for handwritten letters of application with an accompanying CV to be required. Unlike employers in the maintained public sector, some Independent Schools have continued to see value in a traditionally written letter of application, presumably to provide evidence of the applicant's handwriting style and, in some cases, the possibility that the handwriting may be subjected to interpretation by a graphologist.

In all cases, an application for a first post should explain in no more than two sides of A4:

- why the applicant has chosen teaching as a career, with specific reference to having a positive impact on children's learning and enjoyment of school, backed up by two or three well chosen examples;

- initial training experiences and what has been learned from them to take into the induction year as a classteacher;

- previous experience that is relevant to the role of teacher;

- aspects of the job that the applicant wishes to develop in their first year or two;

- how the applicant will be an impressive professional and what they will bring to the life of the school as a community (for example, a willingness to run an after-school club).

How to structure your supporting statement

Opening paragraph. Say something about you: why you decided to enter teaching, how much you have enjoyed your course in general terms and, if this is for a 'pool' application, what kind of school you are ideally seeking – large/small/ Faith/Community/Academy/Free (or are you completely flexible?). Whatever you say, explain why you are saying it. Use positive adjectives to describe yourself here for maximum impact (e.g. conscientious, committed, hard-working, open minded, keen to develop professionally and so on), although avoid being excessive. Be open about wanting to work in a school that is supportive of NQTs in terms of induction and the quality of mentoring it might offer you from experienced teachers.

Second paragraph. Outline in brief the nature of your teaching practice placements (including the year-group/s taught), what you enjoyed, what you found to be challenging and, vitally, how you learned from these challenges. Be confident here but avoid using expressions, such as 'I believe/I find . . .', which could, if over used, imply to the reader that you are narrow-minded or arrogant (i.e. somebody who thinks they know it all). Remember, you are a beginning teacher at this stage and recruiters will be impressed by evidence of ability and potential that is tempered with a little professional humility. Make it clear, though, that you have learned a great deal from these experiences and that you can take this knowledge into your first year as a NQT.

Third paragraph. Relate the previous paragraph to this one to explain your basic understanding of the 'essentials' of classroom practice: inclusion, classroom management, creating a climate of fun, curiosity and learning, differentiation for children of all abilities (including the most able), using the school's behaviour policy positively and consistently and so on. If possible, give one or two examples from your teaching practice placements to relate this part to your experience gained so far. Again, avoid using empty, waffling phrases such as 'I believe . . .'

or 'In my experience . . .'. Remember, you do not at this stage have very much experience. To be blunt about it, most NQTs do not really know what they believe in any detail at the early stages of a teaching career, since it takes years to develop real insight and deeper understandings of cognitive processes, and too many applicants put this kind of rhetoric in their statements, which weakens the statement and sounds hollow. Rather, stick to two or three solid examples from your teaching practices, explaining that you have found them to be effective in promoting children's learning, and why this was the case.

Last paragraph. Finally, reiterate your commitment and determination to do well as a beginning teacher, yet still with much to learn, but with a good deal to offer as a professional who enjoys working with children and seeing them develop in broad terms. Here, showing a little humility while sounding confident will make your statement ring true and sound individual. Add a sentence if you have already supported or run an extra-curricular club in your practice schools (we hope you have!) saying that you will be fully involved in the extra-mural life of the school community to foster children's social development and interests outside the classroom, words to the effect that if appointed you would give your full commitment to achieving well in your crucial NQT year and beyond. End with a final sentence expressing your thanks for the school's consideration of your application.

As this book goes to print, it is still very much a 'buyers' market' in some areas; in other words, schools can usually pick and choose from several applicants, so your application has to exude 'quality' to any potential employer. In schools where NQTs are well supported, they get a lot from the induction year, but such schools expect a lot in return, tending to interview only those applicants who show in their forms the right balance between confidence, raw talent and a little humility in recognising that they still have a lot to learn, and yet have great potential as teachers. Finally, make sure your English (spelling and grammar) is perfect. Most Headteachers and governors will resist interviewing anybody who can't spell, punctuate, express themselves clearly and succinctly or use the apostrophe correctly. Make sure you ask at least two people in whom you have absolute confidence to proofread your application form and supporting statement, taking any criticism with good grace and a positive attitude.

Tips for the application form itself:

1   Use black ink.

2   Type or write legibly in your best hand.

3   Account for all periods of time post-16 (leave *no* gaps whatsoever). If you have had a period of unemployment or a 'Gap Year', you must state this and explain succinctly how you spent your time (e.g. August 2013 – June 2014 Gap period following university, spent travelling abroad).

4   If a section on the form does not apply to you, write 'N/A' (Not Applicable).

5   Include all grades for examinations post-16 (for example 'A' Level grades or Certificate/Diploma grades). Include GCSE passes at 'C' or above, although these do not need to include subject grades unless, having a set of As, you really want to draw attention to them – this might be good where the A grades have been gained in English, mathematics and/or a science. Of course, a pass at Grade C or above will have been a requirement in English Language, mathematics and a science subject for matriculation onto your course of ITT (Initial Teacher Training), wherever it has been undertaken in the country.

6   In the section set aside for your supporting statement, write 'Please refer to enclosed A4 sheet' and print the statement using the following guidelines:

  –   one to one and a half sides of A4 only;

  –   Arial font, point 11 or 12;

  –   right justification

  (these are just our suggestions which you may choose to follow. Individual applications may specify other formats.)

7   Give full contact information for both referees: one should be your ITT tutor and the other the Headteacher or mentor in your final teaching practice school (personal references from friends and associates are not acceptable). Ensure that you request permission from referees before giving their names. It is also useful to talk to them about the nature of the post you are applying for so that they can structure their comments appropriately.

8   Sign and date the form at the end – be sure to sign the section requesting Disclosure and Barring Service (DBS) safeguarding disclosure.

9   It is not mandatory to complete the Ethnic Minority monitoring form that most LAs attach to the application, but it could look a little contrary if you refuse to complete it.

Making applications for promoted posts

When it comes to making an application for a promoted post, much of the aforementioned still applies, although there will be some significant differences. By the term 'promoted post', we mean a second or third job on the promotional ladder, perhaps as a Key Stage Leader, Core subject leader or SENCo, which usually comes with an additional payment in the form of a TLR. Such posts can also be seen as middle-management opportunities and it is usual for any prospective Deputy Head to have moved through this stage prior to taking on the more senior role (we discuss this shortly).

Being successful in the first promoted post is vital since it will be the first opportunity to contribute significantly to the work of the school and the standards achieved across every year-group. With positive recognition for having an impact on standards, the aspiring teacher's confidence is edified and this often leads on to a clearer picture about where to put one's career energy next, either as Assistant or Deputy Head in the same school or elsewhere. The key to making a successful application for a middle-management post is relatively uncomplicated, provided the applicant already possesses the right professional credentials for the job. In essence, the shortlisted applicant will have:

- shown in their application that they have developed the range of skills expected of an accomplished teacher;
- explained how previous subject co-ordination work has prepared them for a more significant whole-school role;
- proved, through reference to some examples and, ideally, hard data, how their teaching has had a positive impact on children's progress and attainment;
- suggested through the application that they have the ambition and potential to aspire to whole-school leadership;
- matched the application very closely with the person specification – this last point is vital.

As with an application for an NQT post, the form should always be accompanied by a supporting statement outlining these things in the applicant's professional profile. Apart from being word perfect (which at this level must be the assumption), the statement needs only to be one or two sides of A4 since an essay is likely to be viewed as waffle or overkill on the part of the applicant. It looks professional, also, if the whole application is prefaced with a short letter stating that the application is enclosed and is matched to the job specification. At this level, any flaws in an applicant's application will usually mean rejection before the interview stage.

The content of the supporting statement need not extol the value of education and learning *per se* since, unlike the beginning teacher trying to persuade the selectors that he or she is vocationally suited to teaching, this will be a given for the experienced practitioner. Instead, the substance of the statement should convey a convincing track record of professional achievement to date, coupled with high personal standards, and how this has had an impact on children's learning or the success of the class and school. These positives need to make explicit reference to the post being applied for and how the applicant will help to take the school forward in the specific role that has been advertised. Even if the post has arisen in the same school and, perhaps, you have been 'encouraged' to apply for it, the application still deserves the same level of care as if it were for a post outside – the application, and what you say in it, will be kept and effectively forms a record of your work and intentions. Therefore, it is wise never to underestimate the ramifications of any written statement that you make as you progress in the job, however inconsequential it might seem at the time.

Applying for Deputy Headship

Those teachers who have made a success of their teaching, and who have taken the requisite steps through middle- and usually a specific senior management role to develop a suitable career profile, will have had Deputy Headship in their sights when an appealing post in a school becomes available. Since, as we suggested earlier, Deputy Headship should really be seen as an apprenticeship ultimately for becoming a Headteacher, the decision to apply will not have been taken lightly. Therefore, to maximise the chance of being shortlisted for interview, the written application must be both impressive professionally and exemplary in its execution.

Unlike other promoted posts below the level of Deputy, this role will require the post holder to become involved in whole-school management and improvement in the broadest sense. Therefore, the successful applicant will have to be able to demonstrate through their application that they have solid achievement behind them and the potential to aspire to a Headship of their own in time. The job specifications for Deputy Headship always make plain this very full skill set and often run to several sides of A4. The main areas under which each element of the specification is subsumed usually reflect the major facets of school organisation: curriculum, teaching, assessment, leadership, finance, working with others and so on. The supporting statement must make a tangible link to the specification, addressing each 'essential criterion' with hard and relevant evidence of achievement and, ideally, meeting most if not all of the 'desirable criteria' as well.

It is very important to match the application to these requirements, leaving no omissions where they are stated as 'essential'. A selection panel for a Deputy's post will not just involve the school's Headteacher, but will certainly comprise two or more governors and, quite possibly, a representative from the Local Authority which, if the school is maintained by the LA, has advisory rights in the selection procedure even though this representative will have no voting right in the final selection of a successful candidate. However, the LA would have the right to veto an appointment if the preferred candidate was not appropriately qualified or failed to meet the person specification in any major way. Therefore, the application must convince any number of people, each with their own priority. For the Headteacher, all other things being equal between applicants, this will all hinge on whether or not they think they would be able to work effectively with a candidate. Again, a suggested 'model' statement simply encourages generic and ill-matched text that is bland and undistinguished, so applicants must construct their own argument with direct reference to the job specification, as we have suggested above.

However, it is likely that the statement will give an opportunity to explain, in an individual style, some of the key qualities required for successful Deputy Headship and the following ideas and suggestions will certainly help:

- The need for the Deputy to have a clearly identified senior role within the school.

- The value of being an effective leader of staff who can earn respect as the Head's 'executive officer' in his or her own right, not just as somebody who deputises for the Head in their absence.

- Quality of work that is exemplary and that inspires colleagues to strive for their best performance to secure good outcomes for all children – the impact of the Deputy on pupils' learning and their rates of progress is crucial and an applicant must indicate their potential for being a force for the good by providing evidence of their achievements in this respect in their career to date.

- An ability to work in partnership with the Headteacher, encouraging the idea of a 'Headship Team'; two individuals working in a complementary way with strengths counterbalancing weaknesses where there is mutual recognition and respect.

- The quality of being approachable; somebody who will inspire trust from staff, the Head, governors, parents and pupils – somebody who is able to act in confidence and to keep confidences when offered them by others.

- The Head must be able to trust the Deputy to be loyal and supportive. Any point of policy disagreement between Head and Deputy should be privately dealt with and never publicly aired; the Head and Deputy must stand side-by-side if working harmony for the good of the school is to be achieved.

- The Deputy must be able to be trusted by the Headteacher to manage the school day-to-day in their absence and this confidence should extend to staff, governors and the parents.

- As well as shared strategic leadership of the school, the Deputy should have a distinct management role in their own right too, for example curriculum co-ordination, assessment, pastoral, support staff, CPD etc.

- The Deputy should be prepared to identify and take on areas of responsibility that are not covered by existing staff, for example co-ordination of a subject area where no other teacher is available; they should also be prepared to tackle difficult or unpopular jobs from time to time as they arise.

- There may be occasions when the Deputy needs to act as intermediary between the Head and other staff, governors or parents, although this will usually depend on the Head's own management and interpersonal skills.

- The role is essentially a shared one with the Headteacher and should include a prominent role in school self-evaluation and monitoring to support and drive school improvement.

The supporting statement should signal an awareness by the applicant of these attributes, making each clear by reference to a few carefully selected examples from their current role.

The role of Deputy Headteacher is arguably the most complex one in a school, a tough and often long apprenticeship in preparation as a Headteacher. The job varies tremendously from school to school, although one factor in common among all posts is the Deputy's bridging nature of being an intermediary between the Headteacher and the rest of the staff. This introduces potential for conflict if the Deputy is not clear about their pivotal role in the success of the school and, as we have intimated above, this quality should be drawn out through the applicant's statement of support when making an application.

Headteacher applications

For many people, applying for Headship can seem daunting. The decision to go for a post usually follows some lengthy soul-searching during which time prospective Heads ask themselves whether they really do aspire to running a school, and whether they will be able to deal with the inevitable stress and responsibility of being the one where, uniquely in a school, the buck will stop, whatever the situation. They may also wonder if they are temperamentally suited to being a Headteacher. As we said in Chapter 11, nothing ever fully prepares you for sitting in the 'Big Chair' until the first day comes and you become the Headteacher of your own school.

If the prospective Head has enjoyed a good previous experience as a Deputy, being involved in most or all of the various strategic aspects of school management, and if they have been coached and sponsored by their Headteacher, and made to feel confident in their abilities as a leader too, the process of applying for Headship should come as a natural extension to the apprenticeship as a Deputy Head.

While all of the preceding ideas and advice when writing applications continue to apply, an application for Headship needs to demonstrate how Deputy Headship has fully prepared the candidate in all major aspects of school management and curriculum leadership to enable the new Headteacher to articulate their *vision* of Primary education in the specific context of the post for which application is being made. Whereas an application for an NQT post or first promotion would not normally include exemplification of the candidate's philosophy of child development and how Primary education promotes this, an application for Headship will require at least an overview of the candidate's educational philosophy and how this will bring success to the school itself. In doing this, the application and supporting statement must pay impeccable attention to the detail of the person specification, referring to each element in turn and how the applicant has either achieved this in their current post or how they would do so if appointed. Again, writing a cogent statement that focuses on the job itself, backed up by evidence rather than mere assertion (and avoiding waffle or repetition) is key to gaining the selection panel's attention when it decides who is to be shortlisted for candidacy.

Although each LA will have its own style of application form, most will specify key areas that applicants must address if they are to be considered as eligible to apply. Aside from qualifications and Qualified Teacher Status, there is usually space on the form for the applicants to explain their skills and abilities, their professional knowledge, experience, ability to work with others and so on. It is a matter of preference whether applicants complete these sections rather than submit a separate A4 sheet although, if the preference is for a typed A4 sheet appended to the form, the statement should directly reference each section of the form using the precise section titles used by the LA.

One common error in unsuccessful Headship applications is a tendency for the applicant to catalogue the many responsibilities inevitably held over the years along with initiatives overseen or introduced by the individual as teacher, middle leader and Deputy Headteacher. What a list is likely to omit is evidence of the impact of this work on children's achievement and the improvement of the school, however specific this may be. Headship applications must include evidence of improvements led, or supported by, the applicant that can be corroborated by reference to data in whatever form these take, whether as assessment data, SATs results, Ofsted reports, pupil surveys and so on. Applicants must at all cost avoid any charge of empty assertion in their application statement if they are to be considered as a viable candidate for interview.

Since the Headteacher's role is to some extent the absolute one in a school, the application must be flawless in its language, grammar, content and style. It must address the person specification directly in every respect and withstand the scrutiny of the Governing Body and Local Authority Adviser, who will certainly be involved in the shortlisting process if the school is maintained by the LA and also in Academies and Free Schools, too, if professional advice is sought from the LA by the school's Governing Body. Therefore, it has to be faultless, convincing and persuasive. If achieved, solid applications will result in invitations to attend interviews, during which the selection tests described in the next chapter will need to be accomplished before an offer of employment is made.

Applications in general

We said at the start of this chapter that there is much common ground in applications for teaching posts at every level. One thing we would urge you to avoid above all others, whatever post you are applying for, is the use of jargon and clichés in the text of your statement. For some reason many applicants feel that their case is enhanced by the use of hackneyed words and phrases such as 'empowering', 'embedding', 'vision', 'developing the whole child', etc. Our experience is that this is not the case and those reading the applications glaze over when confronted with this sort of language and quickly pass on to more focused applications. The advice is that these expressions are meaningless in the context of a specific application and frequently may only serve to irritate some of the selection committee and to make the applicant appear shallow and trite and short on original thought.

Summary and action

All application forms and supporting statements, whether for a first, second or senior post, must be carefully written, using correct grammar, punctuation and a clear writing style. The sole purpose of the written application is to secure an interview as a shortlisted candidate for the post. Applications for first teaching posts should principally demonstrate the applicant's commitment to teaching through reference to evidence of professional learning and knowledge gained in teaching practice placements. For second and promoted posts, greater emphasis should be given in the application to being an 'expert' teacher supported by evidence of children's achievement through skilful classroom management and a demonstrable commitment to the wider school community as a co-ordinator and/or middle-manager of a specific aspect of school organisation.

For Deputy Headship applications, the key is giving the message that the applicant's track record to date has given them the requisite skills and experience to share in the strategic leadership of the school as well as being a role model as a teacher to the staff. Aspiring Deputies need to show that they have potential as Headteachers too.

Applications for Headship need to show how experience and achievement as a Deputy demonstrate the potential to lead a school successfully since prospective Headteachers are expected to be able to articulate a vision for education based on a combination of experience and forward-thinking; they must be able to convince the selectors that they have the ability to lead the continuous improvement of the school.

In all cases, applications must make specific reference to the job (or person) specification, giving evidence showing that the selection criteria can be met. All periods of time, in employment or not, must be accounted for post-16 with no chronological gaps in the application form. Always ask somebody with a high level of literacy to proofread both the application form and supporting statement: the form can be completed in black ink, although the statement may also be typed on up to two sides of A4, using a plain font such as Arial point 12 (up to three sides for Deputy Head or Headteacher applications). Sign the application form and Declaration section at the end in black ink and write a short covering letter to accompany the form stating which post you are applying for and making brief reference to the contents of the application and your suitability for the post as advertised.

13

The interview

The final hurdle

In teaching, applications for any sort of job, whether for a first appointment or a second Headship, culminate in an interview. The content and rigour of the process may be different and the number and type of the supplementary tasks that form part of the final selection process may change, but there will be no escape from the basic experience.

This chapter will help you successfully through the process. It will reassure you that most find interviews a challenging and demanding ordeal and, for some, they are terrifying experiences, but they can be made more manageable. Although each interview is different, certain features are common and particular questions appear regularly, even if in a varied form. Preparation, both for the interview itself and for the other testing experiences that may accompany it, is therefore essential.

Before you go

Invitations to interview for teaching posts sometimes arrive with very short notice. If you have a week or less to prepare, things can be difficult. Fortunately many of the tasks and questions can be anticipated, and the more interviews you have attended, the less likely you are to be surprised by what you are asked to say or do. Prepare for possible questions and think about the way you will reply. Ask others who have had similar interviews for their experiences, and look on the Internet at examples of typical questions. You may even find the interviewers have done the same! In addition to getting ready for the interview itself, you can also do things to prepare yourself for the range of tasks that may also form part of the selection process on the day. These days, for most posts, even a first appointment, you will be lucky to experience just the short interview that was customary for previous generations of teachers, and your skills and qualities are likely to be tested in other ways. According to the nature and level of the post you are being interviewed for, the tasks you can be given can extend over a whole day and will fall into a number of categories:

- teaching activities/taking an assembly
- presentation
- paper exercises
- data analysis
- meeting groups of staff, governors or children
- the final panel interview.

This chapter will consider each of these in turn and suggest ways in which you can prepare to meet the variety of challenges they present.

Teaching activities

There is now a widespread practice when appointing classroom teachers, even at a senior level, of observing them teaching a lesson as part of the selection procedure. If practical, the Headteacher or another senior member of the staff will arrange to visit the schools of all the shortlisted candidates and sit in on a typical lesson. From the appointing school's point of view this is a sensible safeguard since, despite what is said in references, a teacher might not come up to the standard wanted and, once appointed, can prove difficult to deal with. Visiting a candidate in their own school can reveal a lot about how they teach, relate to children and organise their classroom in a way not possible in the course of an interview.

For the candidate, of course, it's a stressful addition to the application process, but, if you have to be observed, there is a big advantage to this type of visit. You are on your home territory, with children, facilities and surroundings you know well. The lesson being observed will form part of your planned routine, added to which you can sometimes arrange to have any challenging children removed or supported during the lesson. You will be used to being watched. Even experienced teachers regularly have observers at the back of the room, so it's not the daunting prospect it once would have been. The advice here is, just do your job, treat it as normally as possible, and try to ignore the presence of anyone else. They might feel more uncomfortable than you do. This approach is time consuming for the appointing school and may sometimes be prevented by the distances involved.

More difficult to deal with is the requirement for you to attend for interview at a school and, in addition, during the day, teach a lesson to a group of their pupils. Here, you will not know the children, their ability, the resources available, or normal school practices, and you will be flying blind with probably little time to arrange and set up the classroom as you would wish. You will be dressed for an interview, which may not be entirely suitable for the classroom activity you have been asked to undertake. It may be also that, in this situation, there is more than one observer. This will be the same for everyone else and, if there is an internal candidate who would have a clear advantage, the interests of equal opportunities should rule out this type of observation.

If you are to be observed in the host school, you should be given information in advance about what is expected. You will be told the age group of the children and there should be an indication of the group size, what activity you are expected to teach, and for how long. Prepare as best you can in the time available, taking advice from colleagues and, where possible, using lesson ideas you are familiar with and have used before. Use straightforward tactics and avoid too much sophistication. Always introduce yourself to the group and establish the names of the children, perhaps using sticky labels to help you remember who they are, as this is likely to impress. Keep to the allotted time and try not to introduce anything too elaborate or complicated, especially if it involves IT, which can let you down at the last minute and leave you floundering. Don't forget the lesson objectives and success criteria and a copy of your plan for the observers!

What is really being assessed here is the way you interact with children, your teaching style and whether you will fit into the team. In a short period with an unfamiliar group of children in an alien environment, it would be very unrealistic to think that an observer could make fair and reliable judgments about your overall teaching ability. They are trying to get a flavour of how you work and compare it with other candidates who are in the same position.

For some more senior posts, especially prospective Heads and Deputies, the teaching challenge can take the form of leading an assembly. Unless you have never done this before, it should not be too difficult to plan and carry out and it will not involve more than a representative sample of children because other candidates have to do the same thing. You may be asked to bring along some artefact of your own choice to talk about, or be given a topic common to everyone else. Once again, the key is planning, and if you get the chance, try it out at your own school first. Do not run over time and, unless you are brilliant at *ad lib*, stick to your prepared script, but try to build-in some pupil involvement since this is always seen as a good thing. You could find you have a larger audience of adults for this, as some governors may attend as a way of being involved in the process.

Presentations

A presentation to senior staff and governors is an activity that commonly features in the selection of Deputies and Heads, less so for other posts. Candidates are given a topic in advance and asked to talk on it to a panel of governors and professionals for a fixed time. Allocated topics usually consist of issues of special relevance to the school, e.g. how you would raise attainment in maths, or what steps you would take to improve attendance. Although your experience of presentations of this type will vary and you will accordingly feel more or less comfortable about the exercise, we suggest a few guidelines to help you succeed.

- Prepare well and rehearse your presentation in front of someone you trust to comment critically and realistically.

- Try not to overdo the use of PowerPoint. It may help, but many of those watching will be immune to its attractions and gimmicks and would rather see you using your own talents. If you do use PowerPoint, always face your audience and resist the temptation to turn to the screen and read out what is written (have a laptop screen in front of you and use it as a teleprompt). Remember, there is always the possibility of an IT failure so have a Plan B.

- Don't over-generalise. Link your topic to the school concerned as much as you can. Refer to school-specific data and other information you have gathered from research. Avoid jargon, explaining unfamiliar terms, without patronising, to non-education professionals in the audience.

- Don't be afraid to re-arrange the furniture if it helps your technique. It's your presentation, so do it how you want. Decide whether you are more comfortable standing or sitting. Avoid moving about too much since it can be distracting.

- Make sure all of your audience can hear you, see you and feel involved. Build-in the chance for questions about what you have said and try to anticipate what they might be.

- Only use a handout if it really helps to clarify your presentation and adds value. The problem with handouts is that you have to decide whether to give them before you start or afterwards. Each has its drawbacks.

- Keep to the point and stick to time. Nothing is much worse than being told by the Chairman of the panel that you have to finish before you have completed what you want to say.

A variation on the presentation theme, which is becoming more widespread for first appointments, is the requirement to read to the panel from a children's book. The candidate is asked to assume the panel are children and to act accordingly. If you are allowed to choose your own book, choose carefully. Avoid very popular books, which other candidates may well have chosen, and which the panel may already have heard several times, and rehearse before hand. This part of the assessment is designed to judge how you would present to children, so make sure there is plenty of interaction and questions, try to be as uninhibited as possible, and don't be shy of treating your audience like children!

Paper exercises

Typically, paper exercises, which are usually given to candidates for senior posts, exist for two reasons. First, they are a way of assessing your literacy (after all you could have asked someone else to complete your application and you might be dreadful at spelling or grammar!). Second, they are used to judge how you would respond to any number of events that could arise in the course of the school day (The In-tray Exercise).

You may find you are asked to draft a response to a letter from a parent, e.g. a complaint about bullying or incompetent teaching. Apart from the obvious requirement for the letter to be well-written and courteous, the panel will be considering the way you have responded. Is it professional? Are you conceding or judgmental in the absence of evidence, dismissing or accepting the allegations without further investigation? Is your manner unconditionally supportive of any staff named, or are you strictly neutral? Do you offer a meeting to discuss the complaint further? Do you give a timescale for further response? Because you can anticipate, to some extent, the type of written exercise you might be given, you can rehearse some generic responses before you attend and will be able to seek the views of others on their suitability. A model letter does not have to offer a final resolution to the issue; rather, it has to comprise a suitably professional response and make clear what will happen next.

The In-tray Exercise will test your judgment of priorities, the extent to which you delegate appropriately and, because it is often timed, your ability to work under pressure. The most common format is a fictitious list of events, which all happen within a short space of time while you are in charge of the school – teacher absence, missing child, safeguarding issues brought to your attention by a teacher, distressed colleague, a telephone call from Ofsted, a blocked toilet – which you are asked to place in order of importance and explain how you would deal with each. The thing to remember here is that safeguarding and general health and safety matters always come top of the list and, in the case of many of the incidents described, they can safely be deferred or delegated to someone else to deal with. The correct responses can seem a matter of common sense, but some alarming misjudgments have been noted over the years!

Data analysis

Attitudes to this part of the selection process are polarised according to individual experience and aptitude. It is either considered straightforward and easy or looked upon with dread. Once again, we recommend preparation.

Candidates may be faced with an extract from a RaiseOnline document, showing pupil attainment and progress, and asked for their judgments on certain positive and negative trends within pupil groups, or to comment on what they see as key strategic priorities for the future. If you are unfamiliar with

RaiseOnline, it can be an impossible task in a limited time, so it makes sense to look at the one relating to your own school and to attend training on interpretation to help you decipher the data presented. Often training in data interpretation is arranged for Governing Bodies so, if you have access to one, ask if you can attend. It is unlikely that you will have seen this information about the school to which you are applying in advance, although if you have looked online at their Data Dashboard, you will have gleaned some insight into their situation and may have reached your own conclusions about areas of success or concern. It is also possible that you will be presented with an anonymous set of data with which you will have no familiarity, so it's the methodology of interpretation you need to practice.

Meeting groups of staff, governors or children

As part of their selection, candidates can find themselves being invited to meet and to engage in discussions with groups of staff, governors or, as is now common, children. These meetings can be billed as informal gatherings, such as tea or lunch, or may be more formal. Occasionally, for instance, the Pupils' School Council is assembled to allow the children to question the applicants. The value of such events is perhaps debatable and certainly draws into question the objectivity of the appointment process as a whole, with no standard criteria to measure performance against. Such methods are usually justified by the argument that they serve to answer those who say the selection of senior school staff should be more open and involve a wider range of people (frequently referred to as stakeholders). It's doubtful that many candidates appreciate meetings of this sort, largely because of the artificiality of their nature, their susceptibility to subjective views, and the constant awareness that every action and response is being watched and noted. We would suggest that these meetings add nothing to the effectiveness of the selection procedure. The consolation is that it's unlikely that, barring major catastrophes, the outcomes will play a significant part in the final decision.

The interview

Experience suggests that, despite the range of trials and tests that might precede it, the interview is still the deciding factor in appointments. It is possible to do relatively badly in the tasks but shine at interview and still win the job. However, some selection days are now arranged so that those who have proved themselves unsuitable in the course of the paper exercises or teaching activities are told they are not required to stay for the interview. Although harsh, and a trifle humiliating, this does at least mean they are spared the ordeal of an interview that may be doomed to fail before it begins.

We have commented earlier that, despite the variations in the content and depth of the questions and the make-up of the panel, the fundamental dynamics of the interview remain fairly constant regardless of the seniority of the post in question. In short, each candidate faces a series of prepared questions from a panel of professionals and governors, and their responses are judged on merit and compared with those of their competitors for the post. We will look at the types of questions that routinely arise and suggest some ways in which they may be answered. We will also illustrate ways in which you can enhance your chances of making an impression through your appearance and body language.

It has often been suggested that most individuals on an interview panel tend to form a judgment about a candidate within a few seconds of them entering the room, an impression from which it is difficult for them to be swayed. That is perhaps an alarming piece of information and, whether or not it is entirely true or even fair, one that you would do well to bear in mind. If the panel is hoping to appoint a Headteacher, for instance, it is important to them that the person who walks in has an appearance and manner with which they associate that role: authority, dress, bearing, confidence. This rule applies at every level of appointment, so it follows that it is essential to look the part whatever job you are seeking. Whether they know it, or admit it, every member of the panel will have personal prejudices that can serve to influence their decision. These will frequently be irrational and connected to such unrelated and irrelevant things as dress-style, hairstyle, accent, sex, physique; in fact, any number or combination of variables. Perfect objectivity is almost impossible to achieve and some interviewers may even have formed a subconscious view that they want to appoint someone exactly like (or the exact opposite of) the person they are seeking to replace. Although many of the panel will have an awareness of this potential and may be able to play down the effect of bias, it remains an unknown element, almost a lottery, which interviewees can do little about.

However, your appearance and demeanour are things that are most definitely within your control. We've mentioned elsewhere the necessity to dress appropriately and adopt a suitable professional manner. There has to be a balance too in what you say and how you act. Having a degree of gravitas can be a distinct asset, certainly for senior appointments, and you should appear both friendly and businesslike at the same time. Try to be neither too earnest nor too flippant. Although it's valuable to display a sense of humour when appropriate, you have to demonstrate the ability to be serious and thoughtful as well. Smiling too much can be as bad as not smiling at all. Eye contact with the questioner and others (without fixing them with a piercing stare), thinking before you respond, speaking with steady measured tones and varying the pitch and modulation of your voice, all help to set the scene and create an impression on the audience of someone who is self-assured, confident and, above all, professional. Sit comfortably and avoid fidgeting and waving your hands and arms about, but make sure you look periodically at each panel member to avoid the impression of ignoring anyone. Answer questions clearly, concisely and avoid rambling or diverging from the point. And, of course, if you don't understand a question, or forget one of the points it contained, always ask for it to be repeated. The panel will expect this to occur and would rather you clarify that you have answered the question correctly.

The panel

Interviewing panels differ according to the post involved and the type of school. For the most straightforward appointments, those for NQTs and classteachers, they may comprise the Headteacher and another senior manager and possibly a governor. For senior posts there will be a larger representation of governors. For Headteacher appointments, there will be a panel of governors and, in Maintained Schools, a representative of the Local Authority. Voluntary Schools may also have someone from the Diocese or Foundation body in attendance. Only the governors have a vote in the selection of Heads and Deputies, but they are advised by others (LA or Diocese) who, under some circumstances, have a power of veto.

All this means that a panel can range from two to a dozen and, as a candidate, you cannot always tell before you go into the room how many people you will be facing or what their backgrounds or experience are. You will be introduced to each by name but you should resist the temptation to shake hands with each of them. A large panel can be intimidating at first and this is a completely normal feeling. On the plus side, there is the advantage that the decision does not rest with one or two people and should result from serious and informed consideration and discussion of each candidate's performance with a balanced decision being reached.

The questions

It is customary these days, in the interest of fairness, for all interviewees to be asked the same substantive questions. A list of questions will have been drawn up and agreed in advance and the panel may decide on a grading scale with which to mark responses. This can make decisions more straightforward. Ideally the questions will be relevant to the post rather than a random list. There should be an agreed format for the interview so that the questions have been allocated to specific members to ask. Everyone will have a number of questions that they ask sequentially or, alternatively, the questioning may go round the table in turn with each member asking one question before things move on. Occasionally there might be a prior agreement that two or three of those present carry out the majority of questioning, with others limited to asking supplementaries or seeking points of clarification.

Although the questions will be standard for each candidate, there is always the chance of supplementary questions seeking clarification or to challenge your answers. These may originate from any member of the panel and can be unpredictable and sometimes a challenge to cope with. We suggest that the way you handle probing questions can do much to influence the outcome of the interview. If you have a strongly held view or something that you feel should be emphasised, don't feel forced to concede or to change your opinion. They will be looking for strength of character and determination based on clear-headed and self-reliant thinking.

This goes to show there is no standard format. You might hope the questions follow some sort of logical progression, but you can't count on it. The topic may move from curriculum to CPD opportunities and back in a haphazard way.

In the interview, most questions take two forms. First, there are generic questions, that is, those connected to your experience and qualities, or to general school issues, such as safeguarding, inclusion, assessment and curriculum. These types of questions occur routinely and you will come to know what to expect. Second, there are school-specific questions that relate to features and situations unique to the appointing school. These can be harder to predict and will require some insight into the special circumstances of the school. Thinking of the questions in this way should allow you to prepare more constructively and avoid some of the element of surprise.

Below are some of the typical areas of questioning you might expect, together with some suggestions for ways of answering.

Generic

Q General questions about your application form. Enquiry about your job mobility, or lack of it. Reference to any gaps in your experience.

A Lack of mobility illustrates commitment and loyalty, or mobility emphasises desire to broaden experience and progress in the profession. Each move has been planned. In the case of this move, you judge it to be the right time. Acknowledge experience gaps and say what you have done/propose to do to rectify them.

Q What do you understand by the term inclusion?

A Be clear about the meaning in education. If possible cite one or two examples that you have been involved in. Be prepared for a follow-up question on the potential disadvantages to the majority in a class if individual special needs are not properly addressed.

Q General question on safeguarding with possible scenario attached.

A Describe how you would deal with the situation in the context of your school's policy and, if possible, quote from the appointing school's policy, which will be on their website.

Q   How have you prepared yourself for this post? How successful do you judge this preparation has been? Give details of any training undertaken.

A   Give some examples of work you have already done that is in line with the job description. (e.g. performance management, observations, leading CPD). Difficult to judge effectiveness as you haven't done the job yet, but you can say that you feel prepared. Outline any CPD you have engaged in as a preparation. Give information about further academic study, Master's degree/Professional Diploma/NPQH.

Q   Is there any area of the curriculum you feel apprehensive about teaching?

A   No harm in admitting as long as you qualify your answer by describing what steps you have taken to deal with your concerns – CPD etc. No one can be good at everything.

Q   How do you rate your communication skills/working relationships?

A   Really for others to judge, but, from your experience of people coming to you for advice and support, you would say good/excellent.

Q   How do you go about earning and retaining the respect of your colleagues?

A   Working hard, doing a good job, being supportive, listening to problems, knowing where to go for solutions. Not expecting others to do something you wouldn't do yourself. Doing what you say you are going to do.

Q   General question on leadership. What is your style?

A   Rehearse a suitable concise definition and describe how you fit it. Describe your strengths. Prepare one or two examples that show you as an effective manager.

Q   How do you ensure your pupils have high expectations of themselves and their work?

A   By personal example and setting exacting standards. Consistency. Critical and constructive feedback through marking. Target setting.

Q   What ideas and strategies do you have about improving the quality of teaching and learning? How would you monitor this quality?

A   Lesson observation with purposeful recommendations for improvement. Model lessons from exemplars. Shared teaching. Effective assessment. Supportive mentoring and coaching of others with clear improvement objectives.

Q   What do you consider makes successful performance management?

A   Describe your experiences. PM should be about stimulating improvement and recognising success. Success is measured by results and the impact on the quality of education for the pupils.

Q   How do you make sure the people you are leading are motivated and clear about their roles, responsibilities and accountability?

A   Shared purpose and values. Holding others to account and confronting poor performance. Teamwork and a common desire to achieve better outcomes. Importance of dialogue and coaching others to improve.

School-specific

Q   How do you think your skills and experience will benefit this school?

A   Pick out features you wish to highlight among your strengths and relate them to a specific area of development or priority you have identified in the school.

Q   What is your view of the biggest challenge facing this school over the next x years?

A   As above. Pick out a few major issues and link them to your particular skills and experience. Be careful not to be too critical of the school or leadership.

Q   If you were to hear negative comments from parents about the school (or from staff about leadership) how would you respond?

A   Stress loyalty and support. You would hope that as a manager (if appropriate) you would be party to decisions affecting the school and would therefore understand fully the strategies involved. Collective responsibility. Obviously it might be necessary to intervene or report to others. (If not a senior teacher it would not really be your place to comment).

Q   As a senior manager, how would you deal with a member of staff who was showing a lack of competence and struggling with their job?

A   Support and sympathy. If necessary the competency procedure would need to be invoked after attempts at support have failed. Need to see what factors were contributing to underperformance (health, domestic, stress).

Q   Question about community involvement/PTA.

A   Describe any involvement at your present school and then relate your answer to what you know of community involvement at the appointing school.

Slightly pointless

Q   Why have you applied for this post?

A   Career development, suitable opening, like the school, etc.

Q   What do you see yourself doing in five years' time?

A   How can you tell? Your response has to suggest ambition, but not give the idea that you will be gone in no time, or are immodest. If you are doing further study you could relate your answer to that. Depends what they are looking for.

Q   What are your strengths and weaknesses?

A   Good chance to outline strong points, but you are not going to be honest about serious shortcomings if you are aware of them. One strategy is to select a good point (e.g. obsessively punctual/meticulously tidy) and label it a weakness, although canny and experienced interviewers may well be wise to this.

Q   What makes you angry?

A   You are not going to admit to an uncontrollable temper so either say 'not much' or highlight something that would make anyone angry.

Q   Why should we offer you the job rather than any of the other candidates?

A   Difficult to answer as you do not know the other candidates or their qualities. As far as you are concerned you are an excellent candidate matched against the job description, and have suitable qualities, that is why you have applied.

Inappropriate

The Chairman should not allow these, but if they slip through and you feel obliged to answer we recommend as follows. Questions about religious practice may be acceptable in the case of appointments at Faith Schools.

Q   How will you balance the demands of the job with the role of mother? Have you made suitable child care arrangements? Or, do you anticipate having children in the near future?

A   I have always succeeded in keeping my private and professional life separate so that one does not disadvantage the other.

Q We are looking for someone to stay in this post for x years. Are you prepared to do that?

A I cannot give guarantees about the future as no one is able to foresee what will happen in the future.

Q You currently live a long way from the school. Are you prepared to move nearer?

A Where I live impacts on my family as well as me. If I felt my domestic arrangements were disadvantaging my work, I would seek to do something about it.

After it's over

Expect to be told the outcome of your application soon after the last interview. Sometimes candidates are asked to wait outside, which can be an ordeal. Other times they will receive a telephone call, usually the same day. When a job offer is made to the successful applicant an acceptance is expected. This constitutes a binding commitment on both parties.

Unsuccessful candidates may be offered feedback on their performance. This can be useful, although it may simply be a case that the winner was considered to be better than everyone else. If there are points raised about ways to improve performance in the tasks you undertook or the interview, take note of them and try to act on them before the next interview.

Summary and action

Selection procedures often involve a number of tasks in addition to the more traditional interview. These can be written exercises, presentations or teaching activities. You can prepare for these in a number of ways. Interviews themselves have certain common features irrespective of the level of the appointment. Questions fall into categories and, like exam questions, can be researched and anticipated and suitable responses practised. With adequate preparation and a little luck you should not be surprised.

Interview panels comprise professionals and governors, who will not necessarily have technical knowledge, and can vary in number according to the appointment. Members can have personal prejudices and can be influenced by appearance and demeanour as well as answers to questions.

Key actions

- Prepare carefully for presentations and teaching activities and seek advice from others on what you plan to do and say. If you plan to use IT always have a back up handy. Keep to time and never overrun.

- Anticipate some of the content of written exercises and prepare possible responses.

- Look at lists of possible interview questions appropriate to the post you are applying for and work on your planned responses. Be prepared for challenges to your answers and expect follow-up questions.

- At interview, take care with your body language and strive to appear confident, knowledgeable and professional throughout.

- Become familiar and comfortable with RaiseOnline and ways of interpreting school performance data.

- If you are unsuccessful and receive feedback, act positively on any advice you are given.

Epilogue

A path well trod . . .

Assuming that you have found this handbook useful in its intention of helping you to contemplate and to plan your career, you are likely to have come to this point from a number of perspectives: the trainee or beginning teacher with your whole teaching career ahead of you; the second jobber, with some teaching experience under your belt, perhaps looking for specific ideas to help you win that first step on the promotional ladder; the returner-to-teaching, likely to be considering your options following a period of maternity leave or a geographical move; the middle leader on the cusp of taking on Assistant or Deputy Headship; the Deputy now feeling ready to start thinking about taking on your own Headship; or even perhaps the experienced teacher, Deputy or Head who is considering jumping off this occupational pathway (some might view it less romantically as a conveyor belt) and thinking about an alternative career making use of your experience in teaching up to this point, not we hope with a negative mind set, but in order to try something new and exciting more widely in the world of education.

Whatever your current situation, we have tried throughout to encourage and to show you how to plan your next step by making your present role successful. However, we have also urged you to think not just one but two, three or more possible steps ahead in your teaching career, encouraging you to keep an eye on your own professional 'career clock', so to speak, in order to allow you to make key decisions about what it is that you wish to achieve at the optimum points in a finite working life. It is worth noting here that ten, twenty, thirty or more years in teaching whizz by at an alarming rate. In other words, we would suggest you 'model' mentally possible scenarios, options and opportunities as you see them while applying a speculative time scale to these ideas. The passage of time in teaching is emphasised by the nature of the academic year, punctuated as it is with fixed term dates and holidays, making it seem to pass more quickly than many might think!

The point we are making is that you will enjoy greater career satisfaction if you keep an eye on your 'career clock', making conscious, informed decisions about career moves, if any, as you progress through the system. You will also benefit from keeping in mind the key stages in your working life, based on your age when you begin teaching, by which you aim to achieve these things. This is not for a moment to suggest that a conventional career trajectory of frequent movement and promotion should necessarily be your main criterion for judging career success as a teacher: you might be content to work in one school as a committed and inspirational classteacher for many years. In fact, many of us probably remember some of these teachers as being those we admired and liked the most. This is why the metaphor of the career conveyor belt or escalator can sometimes be so unhelpful, even in some cases demoralising. Not everyone wants to keep moving upwards nor should they be expected to do so.

There is, though, frequently an expectation among our teaching peers that the sole measure of vocational success is the steady climb up the career ladder, or *the path well trod* that we refer to here. We would argue that this should certainly not always be the case. That said, the conventional career path that measures success by seniority and status alone can be a difficult one to steer away from, such are the pressures of others' expectations of us and, of course, the hook of maximising our incomes within the possibilities of what it is that we do for a living. Schools contain many burnt-out senior leaders, yearning for early retirement that used to be – but sadly is no longer – actuarially enhanced to a full pension at age 55 or so. Such opportunities for people to call it a day are now relegated to history with the advent of increased pension contributions, a higher retirement age (from 60 to 65 for teachers who qualified after April 2007) and early retirement almost beyond question. This means that the older members of the profession will gradually begin to cause a log jam in the system, making for fewer opportunities for the younger generation of teachers to take their place as easily as was the case in the past.

There is also often a mistaken assumption that long-serving 'career teachers' in the classroom are unfulfilled and less admirable than the go-getters who jump and reach for higher plains. Equally, schools are full of people who – had they followed our simple advice to consider and to plan their pathway through the years, one step at a time but with an eye on subsequent possibilities – would feel less professionally frustrated or resentful at the end of their careers as their own options gradually narrow.

In short, the whole thrust of this book has been to urge you to adopt an anticipative approach to developing your teaching career, as opposed to a passive one, simply relying on where you might 'end up' due to other factors; speculatively planning the next step, or steps ahead, through the conscious process of 'modelling' career options in your mind, without being falsely or immoderately ambitious, rather than just letting things happen to you, based purely on serendipity.

We say all of this based not just on our own hard won successes, but also on our own occasional errors of judgment, lack of planning or missed opportunities, despite aspiring to successful Headships of our own and our later work in teacher training in HE. In our own professional cases, it turns out to be true that, 'Life is a Mirror and the Future is a Reflection of the Past' – we want you to gain from our shared experience of the past while not reflecting those missed opportunities from which we have had to learn, sometimes to our cost.

We both wish you good fortune and happiness in achieving your aims.

Index

Printed in Great Britain
by Amazon